Traveler

On
Walking
My
Mother
Home

i

Mark J DeMaio
Son of Anthony and Patricia DeMaio

ISBN: 9781943333189

Front Cover Mandala Design: Alejandra DeMaio
Front Cover, Mandala Digitization and Fill: Wolf Murphy
Book Design: Wolf Murphy
Printed By Lightning Source POD
First Edition Printing 2022

Caravan Learning Incorporated
9907 Piney Point Cir
Orlando, Fl. 32825

www.caravanlearning.org

This work is dedicated to anyone

who has ever experienced loss and grief.

It is especially dedicated to my mom,

who I believe came to and through me

to offer this as a gift.

Mark J DeMaio, January 6, 2022

Table of Contents

Foreword

We are surrounded by death every day we live. Some deaths are relatively easy to face—the meat on our plates, the house plant that we overwatered. Some are larger, overshadowing any living we've ever had to do, making us feel as if we will never be able to crawl out from under their quietus shadow.

How do we face these larger deaths? More importantly, how do we honor a being going through their own death process, while we still can be in life with them? This is the question that this memoir explores, and is why it is essential reading for anyone who will have (or has had) to bear supportive witness to the death of a dearly loved one.

It's no new insight that we, as Americans, face such an absence of culture around the process of death, for both the dying and the soon-to-be bereaved. We struggle to make ritual out of what we can in the unlivable moments where we must rely on some external force to carry us through, where no actions of our own making, make any sense at all. I was discussing my own clinging to various cultures' rites and rituals with a new friend, wondering how much I could whole-heartedly embrace without "culturally appropriating"—the new unforgivable and ubiquitous transgression of the common era. My Hindu friend replied that as long as I had *shraddha*, I needn't worry about cultural appropriation.

Shraddha is originally a Sanskrit word that has no direct English translation, but can be expressed as "acting from the heart, with purpose and deep faithfulness." It is not the notion of "blind faith," but rather is faith born of the certainty that one is acting in accordance with the divine, on the humbling path of devotion to divine truth. This is such a beautiful word to come to me while writing this foreward for Mark's deeply loving, unflinchingly honest account of his experience during his mother's last months, days, and minutes of living. Coincidentally (or not!), *Shraddha* is also the term for the Hindu ceremonial rite performed in honor of a deceased ancestor—especially by a son for his deceased parents—at certain intervals after the death has occurred.

Shraddha requires devotion, respect, humility— essentially, the ingredients of love. Even when his experience is unavoidably painful, Mark comes from this place within these pages, and it is a gift to be there with him. I know that when I am called to bear witness to my own loved ones' passings, I will do my best to carry his example with me.

—*Vanessa Rose, Austin, TX*

Introduction

Culturally, now, we're really tight around death, and as a result I think people miss out on a lot of the beautiful aspects of the end of life process that can be very helpful for the grieving process, that can be a really beautiful part of transition of life that we don't get to experience because it's not in the conversation.

— Chrysta Bell

What begins here is documentation of a process in which I walked my mother home. Whether "home" means to heaven, to god, to the universe, or just to the void that comes in the eternal sleep, I will leave only as something to ponder. This journey started slowly. It progressed as the undeniable and indelible connection to my mom repurposed itself again and again.

As I took control of my mom's affairs as her power of attorney, this connection was only given space by the necessary logistics of lawyers, medicaid application teams, and more. Though I do not wish to focus on that part in this account, I do posit how important it really is to do. I want to first and foremost thank the Olsen Law Firm, Robert Hiddock, O'Rourke & Associates, and the Cameron Group for all their professionalism and assistance.

And as a short public service announcement, we should all do our estate planning sooner rather than later. The last thing you want is your family scrambling when that inevitable time comes, and some family members not in agreement on what it is you wanted. And that time does come for us all, though we like to deny it as a culture. How often do we call someone morose or morbid for thinking or speaking on the topics of aging and death? How often do we disregard the topic for a "later" that never comes to "now"? It's so very important to know what one wants in regards to medical interventions, last rites, and funeral services. It is best to have the time and space to focus on the relationships, the spirit. It's really best to put all that business

1

stuff on autopilot if possible. I have one friend who keeps a file on her phone with all of this information just in case it ever happens—just food for thought.

That aside, I wish to utilize my platform here to explore the emotional journey as a son and father—a generational bridge in an odd time of covid. I started documenting things as a keepsake that I could show my children one day. As this journey was largely private, it was like some annexed compartment of me had a huge foothold that my children could never see. That alone I'm sure shaped this experience in many ways. At some point, I started posting some of my journaling in hopes to keep a record and perhaps offer some insight for others. The feedback was just tremendous. Hundreds of friends would like or comment on each share. People messaged me privately with support and gratitude for what I was doing. One person randomly sent me $111 so I could have some self-care. Others told me personally how important it was that I eventually publish and share this with the world. It just organically happened. It feels as if everyone wants to address the topic of dying and death, but nobody has had the avenue or support to do so. Perhaps my witnessing herein will offer a launchpad for that in others. I hope so.

Looking back through all the material, I quickly realized that I could expand on everything and turn this into a much larger work. I decided that was not what I wanted to do however. It's my hope that this work will be emotionally consuming rather than intellectually analyzed. My love for my mother compelled me to write it. I hope it will provide some insight, that it will be a drop in the larger ocean of compassion, and that everyone it reaches will themselves connect in safety with their own experiences of loss and grief.

There are some entries that are not directly related to the subject of my mother's dying process, but I offer them as a glimpse into the mindset of someone navigating the process. This work was in it's own way a very stream of consciousness experience; a stream of consciousness that spread out over the course of about a year. In many cases, the quotes and posts also relate to the larger philosophical and contextual arc of my own journey which can not exist in a bubble. In subtle and not so subtle ways, my journey relates to my mom's. I hope you will find illumination through these puzzle pieces of my consciousness and also with some notes that have been provided as assistance to timelines and references that you might not otherwise be privy to.

At this time I want to offer my deepest gratitude to Helen for all her support, guidance, and getting *The Prayer for the Dead* to me just in time; to Byron Ballard for the generous permission to use her piece in its entirety; to Alan Watts, Ram Dass, David Whyte and others for helping me meditate on all things related to life, death, and the hereafter; to Rhett for being a thorn in my side when I needed it most; to Charles for the Cosmic Baby; to Christine for that random and beautiful gift of $111; to my sister Loretta for always having my back on the tough decisions; to my brother-in-law Nick for providing all the room and board to keep me going all those long weekends in Gainesville; to my sister Kim for managing things with more grace than maybe she knew she had; to Wolf for being my publisher and designer; to Bonnie for the conversational distractions; and to V for all the editorial oversight, encouragement, and reflection. I also want to thank my children for constantly challenging me, and most of all my wife for inspiring me to find love in everything.

And so it begins . . .

I wish I knew the beauty
Of leaves falling
To whom are we beautiful
As we go?

—David Ignatow

Hail the Traveler

August 28, 2020

A Memory

I called my mom to wish her a happy 82nd birthday. She was a bit cagey and fiery, but that's nothing new. She said there's not much to be happy about and that it's her worst birthday ever. I told her I wish we could visit, but it's not a safe time with all the grandkids and covid raging rampant in Florida. She said maybe covid will get her. She expressed concerns that Joe Biden will come for her money and take it all away. She expressed concerns about other people coming for her money. She expressed concerns that I'll come for her money. I sensed something was off, so I asked her how she'd like me to handle things if she ever lost some of her autonomy. She accused me of calling to piss her off. I told her I love her and just wanted to know. She always did seem to have an uncanny knack for avoiding the topic.This isn't the first time. I imagine many other parents are the same way.

A Memory

My mother was hospitalized with a raging urinary tract infection and an open sore on her foot from diabetic neuropathy. I began taking treks to Gainesville every weekend while she was in the hospital. I spent 6 to 12 hours by her side every Saturday and Sunday. I was able to spend a few hours Friday evenings and Monday mornings as well. It became obvious on my visits that the UTI had created a new baseline for her mind. Dementia had come to visit with a far more robust wardrobe than we had previously noticed. We realized, upon reflection, that some warning signs had been presenting themselves in the months prior. Covid had kept us at some distance for her protection. I pondered in the quiet moments at the hospital if it really protected her at all. I still worried about covid some, but I knew the risk of not being by her side was far greater than the risk of being by her side. I stayed by her side. My sisters did too when they could. She was allowed one visitor at a time. We had to be masked always and our temperature checked at every visit. I got to know the map, elevators, hallways, and shortcuts of that hospital very well.

Note: Pictures are from the area around the Hospital.

An Email to My Siblings

Dear Family,

I know this moment in time is not easy for any of us. I am holding space as much as I can for mom and also trying to integrate the many possibilities of what comes next. I wanted to give you a short update on what I'm seeing here at the hospital.

Mentally
- Mom doesn't know what year it is.
- She thinks her mother died a week ago.
- She can remember many details of the past, but isn't holding onto much new information. For example, if the nurse asks her to shift to the right she forgets the instruction almost immediately. She did, however, remember that I was helping her eat yesterday. She was telling the nurse about it, but she was retelling the story that I had helped her eat for many years.
- She thought her son who was in West Palm had visited the hospital yesterday.
- She speaks to me as if I'm her cat Joseph sometimes. She calls out that I'm being a rapscallion and causing so much ruckus. She wakes up reaching for and kissing out to her phantom JoJo.
- There are moments where she seems more cognizant than others.
- Both the nurse and I noticed she was far more loopy later in the day.

Physically
- She won't cop to it, but she is for all intents and purposes blind. I get that she sees some lights and color and even shapes, but she has no ability to spatially process them or know what they are. She has a lot of trouble feeding herself. She tried to eat a napkin last night, mistaking it for food.
- She currently can't walk anywhere.
- She currently can't stand without assistance.
- Her feet have systemic candida, bunions, and look very bad. There is an open ulcer bleeding on her left big toe, the worst of the two feet.
- She probably has advanced osteoarthritis in her spine. She has a pronounced hump and slouch which surely contributes to her immobility.
- She is eating well.
- She is communicating and is able to know when she needs to go to the bathroom.

I know I'm probably forgetting things, but these stand out.

What comes next?
- She will stay in a hospital bed at least another night. I need to speak to a social worker or transition specialist for what comes next, but I have to go back to Orlando tonight and am currently working online at the hospital. My time is split and challenging.
- The plan for now is that she will go to a rehab center for physical therapy for anywhere from a few days to a few weeks to a whole month. I'm getting different ideas from different sources about how that works.
- Medicare will cover the rehab center so long as they deem mom capable of rehabilitation. I'm not sure how that will play out. I'm concerned they will 'turf' her.

What's after rehab—A list of options:

- Live in home care
- Assisted living facility. Orlando seems the frontrunner on location as I can be more involved there, and it's more central between the rest of you.
- Other?

What do we do now?

- Several of us are searching for options. I'll tour facilities in Orlando as soon as I can.
- Speak to lawyers about any options for protecting mom's assets and property.
- Vote on what we think is the best option moving forward. I can't promise your vote will be what we do, but I do value all your input and want you to be heard and respected.
- Take care of ourselves and feel our feelings.
- Pray or meditate or contemplate or visualize, etc.

Thank you and love to you all,

Mark

September 12, 2020

A Journal Entry

This is the nine year anniversary of my father's transition. I ponder if my mom will join him soon. I observe her eating napkins and having all sorts of difficulty with any basic motor function or conversation.

> You can call me anything,
> but just don't call me late for dinner.
>
> —Anthony N. DeMaio

A Memory

While my mom was hospitalized, I was at her house looking for copies of her last will and testament. While I didn't find what I was looking for that day, I sort of found something better. It was a gift from my dad; my dad's wallet. It was preserved exactly as it had been when he was first hospitalized about a decade earlier. His license and credit cards were there as if he had never left. As I leafed through it, there was only one picture of any of the kids. It was a picture of me. It felt like this was all planned out by him at some higher level of existence; a symbolic gesture from wherever he was now. I knew he wanted me to protect the finances and mom. As that thought crossed my mind, what did I find? Cash! There were still some bills sitting in this beautiful Italian Leather bifold.

I felt my stomach growl. I messaged my sister Loretta a picture of the wallet. She immediately responded that it must have been waiting for me all these years. She told me it was mine and to keep it. My stomach growled again. I cleaned up what I was doing and had a thought spring forth from what felt like beyond my own cognition. "DAD WANTS TO BUY ME LUNCH". I looked at the petty cash and there was definitely enough for a meal. I also looked at the time, and I needed to get back to my mom at the hospital soon. I pondered what dad would have wanted to share with me. The first thought that came to mind was a philly cheesesteak. He was from Philadelphia afterall. I searched for a place nearby. As I arrived, I noticed it was closed. Time was running short. I decided he would have also liked a burger. Since I was in a hurry, I just went to a fast food drive-thru right by the hospital. I ordered a burger and it was delicious. Thanks dad I thought to myself and filed this little story away for later retelling.

Later that day, I did get to retell it. As was becoming tradition the many days I spent in Gainesville, I would leave the hospital when visiting hours were over around seven. I would then stop at my sister's house where her very supportive husband would have dinner delivered shortly after. We'd sit outside distanced on the porch under covid protocols and share a meal. I'd usually get off some steam regarding the challenges of the day and explain what new developments there were in mom's situation. Anyway, I went into my story about the wallet and the lunch and all the little synchronicities. And that was when they asked me which fast food place I went to. I told them. They looked surprised and told me that when dad was in nursing care nearby, he would often loathe the food. At those times, he'd call up my sister and ask if she could get her husband to pick him up a burger from the exact fast food place I had ended up at. It bears repeating, it wasn't even just the same chain—it was the exact same facility. Whoa! I had a story worth telling. Thanks for the burger dad! It was out of this world.

A Quote

The preoccupation with speed is not only confusing, it is often cruel to older people. I spend a good deal of time in Manhattan, where the pace is a barely controlled mania, and have seen how difficult it is for the old to cope with an urban environment. With the cars whizzing by, and the traffic lights changing too quickly, it's difficult for the elderly to take a walk, or cross a street, without being injured (or feeling like a nuisance, at the least). Watching an older woman maneuver with her cane between taxicabs, whose drivers honked at her to move more quickly, I realized the violence done to the spirit of its elderly by our time-obsessed culture.

Medicine is equally caught in the speed-up. When I was a child, doctors were almost a part of the family, making house calls and stopping for tea. Now, at my health-plan visit, I am happy if the doctor and I have time to shake hands and exchange names within the seven or ten minutes that he/she has allotted to see me. The same holds true for lawyers. My nephew, who's a lawyer, tells me he has a special machine hooked up to his telephone to measure every second he spends doing business. Time was, a lawyer didn't bother counting the hours he spent with a client; a lawyer might even share a meal (without charging a fee) with someone whose case he/she was representing. To our time-bent minds, this now seems romantic—almost hokey—but such was the norm in the not-so-distant past.

—Ram Dass, *Still Here*

An email to my siblings

Since the ER, I have either talked on the phone or been in the room with mom every day. I have spent over fifty hours with her in the hospital. Her body and mind need consistent care. It took what felt like a lot of my courage to give her feet a cleaning, scrub, and treatment. I trimmed her fingernails. I sponge bathed her. I shaved her scrubbly little old lady beard. I did these things. Home sounds great in theory, but I have my reservations. She is not a statistic. She has a lot of stuff going on.

That said...

Let's keep moving forward in both directions: homeward bound and long term facility. There is no right decision here. You might think there is, but I am telling you there is not.

Love

Mark

Note: Some stuff edited out for the sake of privacy. One of my siblings was pretty adamant that long term facility care was a bad decision and was wanting us to send her home. This sibling had not visited the hospital and seen her condition in person.

An email to my siblings

L oretta, thank you for everything you have been doing and continue to do to assist with care and concern for mom. I humbly accept the role of power of attorney and will do my best to fulfill the role with integrity.

I know we are all confused about what comes next. I definitely know we are all busy as well. I have put mom on a waiting list at a very highly rated facility in Orlando that is also in a very nice neighborhood. My guess is that would not be any short term solution, but something further down the road.

I hope we hear good news of mom doing well in the rehab center. I call her everyday. It's been very difficult to reach her. She seems to struggle with the phone. Nurses have helped her, but she continues to struggle. I know both Loretta and I have expressed concerns to the facility about mom's inability to use the phone. Once one of us can get to visit, we'll be able to do a practice call with that person in the room so we can learn for ourselves what's going on. I wish we could get a more immediate solution. I feel totally at a loss every time I try to talk to her. I hear a few words and then the phone goes mute for up to minutes at a time. I only seem to catch about ten to twenty percent of what she's saying. I assume she's only catching that much of what I'm saying as well.

Love to you all,

Mark

Note: My mom had now transferred to a rehab center in Gainesville where visiting was very restricted (Thank you covid). This really was a hard time (not that there is ever an easy time) to go through this. My mom's blindness and dementia made using any phone a real uphill battle. In later care, a staff member would hold a phone up so we could do video chats.

A Poem About the Modern Family

From colors bold we circle round
barely a word to say
each fork raised
a knife to the silent ways
The sink water runs to fill
what our eyes allay
And we retreat thereafter to our own devices
We meet with phones, tablets, and vices
a bubble wrapped round the wisest
lest we get dirty and involved
retreat, retreat to the sterile digital walls
enslaved in heartfelt freedom's calls
making miserable love to our own devices
and nothing humans can offer suffices
now huddled up with news of the latest crisis
unaware of these prolonged prices
we pay for our genius devices

—*Mark J DeMaio*

A Post

Ever get so depressed that you give up on recycling?

A Quote

As poets value the sounds of words above their meanings, and images above arguments, I am trying to get thinking people to be aware of the actual vibrations of life as they would listen to music.

—Alan Watts

A Post

Fluidity. The back-n-forth flow of people in sync. The laying down of masks. The invitation to vulnerability. The honest tears of insecurity, fear, loneliness. The belly laughs of knowing someone is so interested in you and your well being that, even in suffering, you can both feel ridiculous, light hearted, loved.

A Post

Every time a patch of forest is bulldozed for a new apartment complex, gated "ticky tacky" homes community, or a strip mall, I find myself feeling angry. I am feeling angry a lot these days.

A Post

Most days are a wild ride of positive and negative, light and dark, contrast. Without contrast, nothing ever comes into focus! And forever we can pick out every blotch in the image and spiral into a fever of loathing and isolation. We can. I don't think we have to. We could also notice the blotches provide the necessary contrast to see other beautiful things in the foreground. My thoughts for the day anyway.

A Post

The struggle is real.

Note: You might notice that my entries don't seem directly related to my mom, but I assure you they are.

A Post

The expression "Who in the world would do something like this?" and all variants thereof were obviously coined by parents.

A Post

Anyone have any feedback on the Lifecare Center of Orlando? Thank you!

Note: I was scrambling to find my mom a place in Orlando before I was scheduled for hernia surgery on November 20th. I had hit nothing but dead ends personally, so I hired an agency to help get her in the door. Ding Ding. That worked almost instantly. It's like you have to pay to get into the club. Lifecare Center of Orlando came up top of their list. I didn't know anything about it and was searching for information. I can imagine anyone else would have done the same. The feedback I received was very positive.

A Post

Do I know anyone with a minivan with seat assist?

Note: I had this image stuck in my mind of taking my mom to the park for riverside strolls in her wheelchair. I envisioned the sounds of my laughing kids playing nearby with picnic lunches, lemonade, and fishing.

A Memory

I transferred my mom from Gainesville to Orlando to be close to me. I didn't know then, but it was to be the last time she would be outside of a facility. I volunteered to drive her from the rehab in Gainesville to the nursing home in Orlando instead of hiring a medical transport service. I did this for a few reasons. Mostly, I thought she'd be frightened by strangers driving her in a medical van for several hours, and I wanted to spend this time with her. It was a long day pulling the straight round trip, but it was worth it.

21

Though she repeated herself fifty times that day, I loved it. She felt so light and happy—like just another weekend drive with her son. I stopped at a fast food joint because I knew she loved their fish sandwich. I stopped just ten minutes from our destination, however, because I was very concerned about her needing to use a restroom. There was no way for me to get her from the vehicle to anywhere really. She could not walk or use the bathroom without assistance. Once we got to the nursing home, it took me a good five minutes with a harness strap and a helper to simply navigate her out of the front seat and into a wheelchair. I could instantly feel her mood shift when she realized where she was headed. The room we entered had a small aviary. The chirping was a comforting sound. We hugged, and I knew I wouldn't be able to see her for a while because of covid safety protocols. She wasn't much for posing for pictures, but the picture above is us waiting for assistance at her new facility. While we ate and chatted, I learned she used to sneak out back as a teenager and smoke her dad's corn cob pipe. I learned it quite a few times. She was definitely into repeating herself. Maybe so am I. Maybe so am I.

A Picture Memory

Note: This was a day before my surgery for a hernia and a forehead mass removal. I had been very anxious to get mom to Orlando before surgery. I was so grateful it just came together a week prior. This particular visit was fortunate as we didn't think we'd be able to see her so soon. After this visit, we were told she'd need more time in quarantine before general population integration. We had to be fully suited up with gloves, aprons, masks, shields, etc just to see her outside for 30 minutes. It was around this time I got a phone that took better pictures. I brought a bluetooth speaker and streamed music from her generation. She complained about the radio station as she put it.

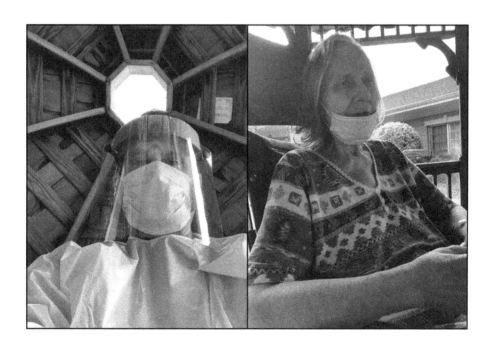

A Post

Recovery underway. No pictures of inguinal hernia (main reason for operation) will be procured. Lol. It's very painful, let me just say. I had a strong reaction to the anesthesia too. Yesterday was a hard one. Today at least my mind feels better. Body is still just a mass of uncomfortable responses to the trauma and the assault of surgery.

A Post

Drums heal!

A Post

The vulnerability that came with surgery has been intense. When they cut you open, you end up cutting yourself open too. It's just part of the introspective process. I've been told by nurses that many men become ill mannered in the hospital because they are so unfamiliar with the inner world, the passive, the sitting still. I get that. I realize I have so much healing to do right now still physically and emotionally. I am waking up in tears almost daily. #normalizementalhealth

Note: Maybe the surgery did something to me. I started to call being put on anesthesia "the little death." I still call it that to this day.

A Random Glimpse Into Parenthood

After I told the boys they should each take a shower, four year old Gabo is undressing. The following dialogue ensued:

Ant (6 years old and speaking desperately): No fair. I want to shower with him, but he won't let me.

Me (trying to problem solve): Ant! You can shower with me.

Ant: Great, I want to do that.

Gabo: I want to shower with you.

Me: Great. Let's all shower together.

Ant (in obvious agony): I JUST WANT TO SHOWER ALONE! WHY CAN'T I JUST SHOWER ALONE?

A Post

Most know my mom went to the hospital, rehab, and a nursing home. I became her power of attorney during all of this pandemic stuff. I also said goodbye to R School, started a completely new hustle with Caravan Learning, went down for surgery, am caring for a slew of kids, and more. We grow stronger I hope. How are all of you doing?

A Quote

To love there must be union with the beloved, but also separation. For love is a creative tension; it is like the string of a musical instrument—a single string yet pulled in opposite directions. If there is too little tension, or if there is too much so that the string breaks, it will give forth no sound. The perfection of love is like the perfect tuning of the string, for love attains fulfillment as there is the maximum of union between two beings who remain definitely separate. Unity in duality is the law of the finite.

—Alan Watts

A Post

While Gabo, aged four, is putting on his hulk night diaper:

> Me: Will you grow up to be as strong as the hulk?
> Gabo: Maybe...if I don't have surgery.

Note: I had been instructing the kids that I could not pick them up while recovering from surgery.

A Memory

Conversations with my mom around this time are often difficult for the family, but I find more ease than most. In her dementia, she invents new memories, inverts or completely forgets original ones, and exists in a dimension of reality apart from our day to day linear consciousness. I want to share one conversation as best I can remember it. It's one of my favorites.

> Mom: I had dinner with Paul McCartney.
> Me: Oh. That sounds awesome. What did you eat?
> Mom: Oh, we had the fixins.
> Me: Was John there too?
> Mom: Yes, I think he was.
> Me: What was his house like?
> Mom: It had many floors.
> Me: Did it have a bowling alley?
> Mom: Maybe it did.
> Me: Did you go bowling with Paul and John, mom?

Mom (laughing with some amusement at the image): Maybe I did.

Me: Did he have a piano in the house? Did you all make any music together?

Mom: Well, I'm too shy to sing in front of anyone.

Me: Ok. What did you all talk about?

Mom: Well, the food and what cars they like to drive.

Me: What cars do they like to drive?

Mom: Well, your dad always liked American cars.

And on and on we'd go—never correcting—never explaining—just exploring the ideas.

A Post

Something I love about my kids is that I am still in bed at 9am on Christmas morning. It's probably the only gift they'll give me this year, but oh what a good one it is.

A Quote

It is well known that under the conditions of various experimental arrangements, light displays either wavelike or particle-like properties. But what, then, is the essential nature of light? This question is not amenable to the usual two-valued logic, and may be better addressed by what is known as four-valued logic, a type of logic that is foreign to and outside of Western thought. Two-valued logic is based on the law of the excluded middle, in which things are either (1) true or (2) false. By contrast, four-valued logic includes the middle and the ends surrounding it, so that things are (1) true, (2) false, (3) both true and false, or (4) neither true nor false.

—Paul Levy

A Post

The sweat rolled down my forehead pooling on my plastic gown covered lap. Only for you mom. See you again next week.

Note: This is when my writing organically started shifting in voice towards my mother.

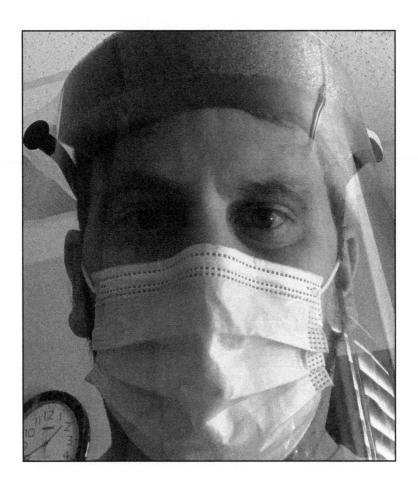

A Post

Ido hope we find the hammers and destroy these halls of mirrors before we become like narcissus—frozen for all time trying to make love to but reflections of ourselves in an endless documentation of great cunning, deception, and design.

A Post

Eventually any musician (I should mention everyone is a musician) who desires to truly connect with others will shun anarchy in favor of collaboration. Anarchy, much like conformity, is another method of control. It becomes at first an appealing counterpoint to the overly-organized rules of polite society, but as the expression says—it is important to not throw out the baby with the bathwater. Music is a mirror for Spirituality in this way—a reflection in the purest sense of Ying and Yang. In the beginning, there was sound. And sound travels infinitely into the cosmos as a vibration from source. And when the source is balanced in collaboration (a 'middle way'), all things flow out from that equanimity.

Song Lyrics

You know that old trees just grow stronger
And old rivers grow wilder every day
Old people just grow lonesome
Waiting for someone to say, "Hello in there, hello"
So if you're walking down the street sometime
And spot some hollow ancient eyes
Please don't just pass 'em by and stare
As if you didn't care, say, "Hello in there, hello"

—John Prine

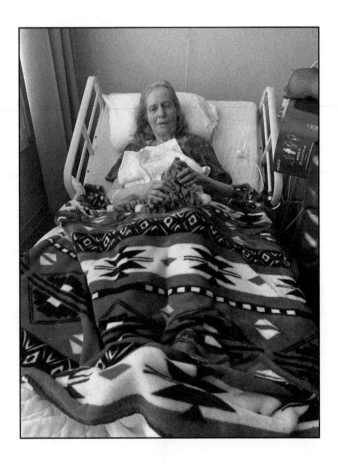

A Post

I have been thinking that trying to colonize another planet to save humanity from itself is like an apple trying to staple itself to an orange tree to escape from the worm that lives within.

A Post

You lost your roommate this week. It must affect the psyche to be so close to someone who dies. You tell me that dad, 9 years gone, visited you today. You shed a tear over the "lady partner" you tell me died. You remain in good humor, but there's plenty of brain fog. Dementia is an iceberg. We listen to the Beatles, cricket noises, and talk about all the dramas of John and Paul and Yoko. I left a haiku for the staff this week. I left some more notes for them as well.

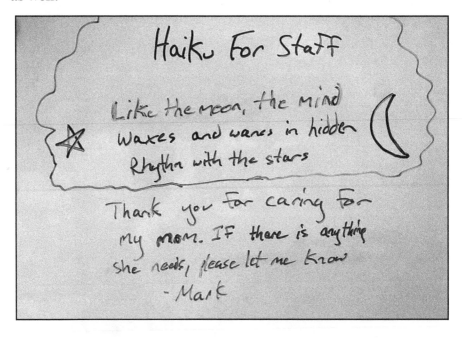

Like the moon, the mind
Waxes and wanes in hidden
Rhythm with the stars

—*Mark J DeMaio*

A Quote

Waking up is a constant. No one is fully awake as long as they are body bound to the material plane. One may be extremely awake to the Truth and live with this Truth as a constant offering. To quote one great sage "GOD is man yet to be fully manifested. Man is GOD yet to be fully realized.

—Michael B. Stone

A Quote

Truth is not something in the distance; there is no path to it, there is neither your path nor my path; there is no devotional path, there is no path of knowledge or path of action, because truth has no path to it. The moment you have a path to truth, you divide it, because the path is exclusive; and what is exclusive at the very beginning will end in exclusiveness. The man who is following a path can never know truth because he is living in exclusiveness; his means are exclusive, and the means are the end, are not separate from the end. If the means are exclusive, the end is also exclusive. So there is no path to truth, and there are not two truths. Truth is not of the past or the present, it is timeless; the man who quotes the truth of the Buddha, of Shankara, of Christ, or who merely repeats what I am saying, will not find truth, because repetition is not truth. Repetition is a lie.

—Jiddu Krishnamurti

A Post

My life will never be as beautiful as your fantasy squares. I know we all are faking it until we make it, and I am alright with that. All my coverings hide scars. I would rather talk about them than sand them down with perfectly hygienic hyperbole.

A Post

Please recommend an accountant that does tax prep for the elderly in nursing homes. I probably need them to help me with my taxes too. Thank you.

A Post

Today we are singing the Beatles together. You have anxiety about people coming to weigh your feet with bags if you don't have your shoes on. You say you are tired of working. I ask you who has the heaviest feet on the block. You say perhaps you do. I call you clubfoot Patty. You laugh for a moment with me. You return to chanting how awful everything is. You cry and ask me if I think I would like doing it. I say no of course not. I organize your clothes and scrub your room with sanitizing wipes. This is hard, but thank goodness for the Beatles.

The one picture is of her in the middle of a song.

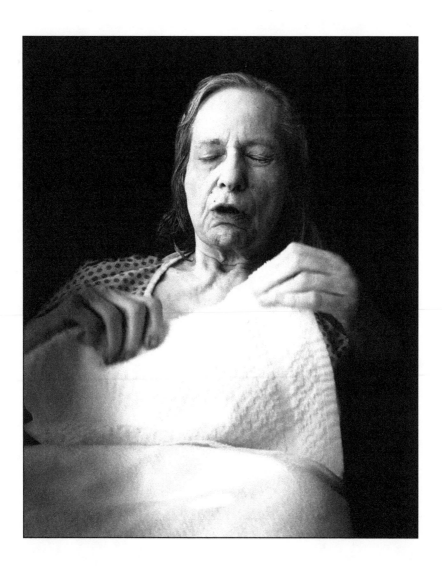

A Quote

Things are as they are. Looking out into the universe at night, we make no comparisons between right and wrong stars, nor between well and badly arranged constellations.

—Alan Watts

The moon in the water;
Broken and broken again,
Still it is there

—Choshu

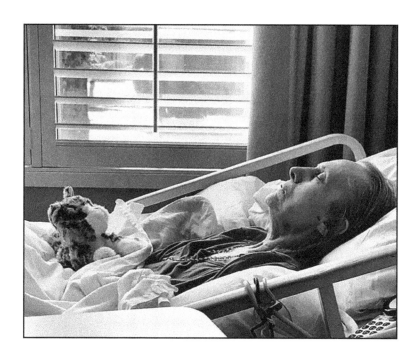

A Post

For two hours today, you slept in silent prayer with a rosary around your neck. I don't know where it came from, but it suits you. You always loved the Catholic Church. Only recently did you curse at god to me in a moment of suffering and existential dread. I told you it's perfectly ok for your faith to waiver with all you are going through. But back to today. I sat vigil for that first hour just watching you sleep and doing my own inner work.

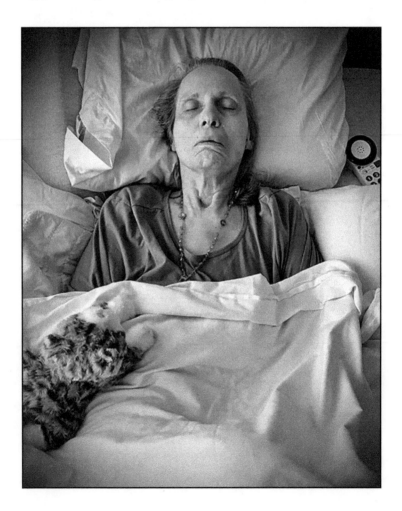

The second hour I wavered and wasted idle time on pointless social media consumption. I wiped down your table and stereo with disinfecting wipes I purchased for your room. The radio was playing an 80's station that kept rhythm to the slow shifts of your breathing. Will you even know I visited? I changed your CD to Abbey Road. Maybe next week we will sing it together. Maybe they upped your anti-anxiety pills without my knowledge. Maybe you're preparing energetically for your next adventure beyond this yellow brick road. I don't know.

I am back to my domestic responsibilities; left pondering how I'll find time to manage your bills, your insurance, your taxes, your home, your spirit. Are you still sleeping now? Are you clawing to get out of the bed? I noticed they put your feet up and several pillows at each side and padded mats around you. I know you cut yourself this week trying to get up. You were disoriented. Dementia and blindness must be one uncomfortably stiff spiritual cocktail. It must make you so confused in space and time. I release you from any responsibility you feel towards me. I still like making you laugh. Maybe I will get a chance next week.

February 21, 2021

A Quote

But poor man! Skillful beyond all other animals, by being able to think in time, and abstractly knowing the future, he dies before he is dead. He shrinks from the shark's teeth before they bite him, and he dreads the alien germ long, long before its banquet begins.

—Alan Watts

A Post

There was no playfulness today. You were in a deep fog, bent over. I thought you might wretch. I put a hospital gown, a bin, and sunglasses on your person. You eventually took the sunglasses off. You mumbled a lot. You have another UTI that's probably fogging you up. The antibiotics probably contributed to your discomfort today.

I left snacks in a drawer for the staff that help you week in and week out. I wiped everything down, and took your companion cat home to sanitize and replace batteries. There is so much more to tell, but I don't have the language to tell it. Today was an absolute test of releasing expectations.

I returned to the parking lot to find a palm tree had made a deposit on my van. It felt like a message, but what is it saying?

For whatever reason, I am left with "there is only the path and you are on the path."

A Post

I am planning to try visiting at a different time. These days you just sleep at 1:30. The snacks I left for staff are all gone and notes were finally scrawled back to me on your whiteboard. That's a success. I replenished the snack drawer and made a note to bring hair ties. That's something I just would not think of, and I am grateful someone thought to tell me. The Beatles were on when I came in, and that lets me know the CNAs are paying attention. I am glad they seem invested in you and your comfort. I will keep feeding them snacks. In a week or so, I will write them a new haiku as well.

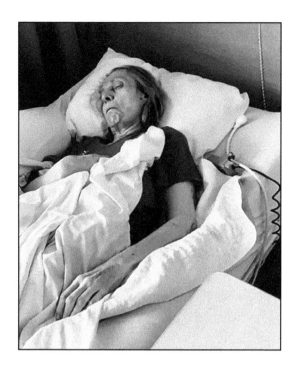

Added Edit: perusing your patient prescriptions files that I monitor now as your POA, I found your official diagnosis—Type 2 diabetes mellitus with hypoglycemia without, Unspecified dementia without behavioral disturbance, Metabolic encephalopathy, Unspecified glaucoma, Essential (primary) hypertension, Unspecified atrial fibrillation, Muscle weakness (generalized), Chronic kidney disease, stage 3 unspecified, Difficulty in walking, not elsewhere classified, Cognitive communication deficit.

You definitely have some things stacked up against you there. I had one person comment on the future that's waiting for me as we were going over your medical history. Oh my!

A Post

Your new roommate was already "gone."

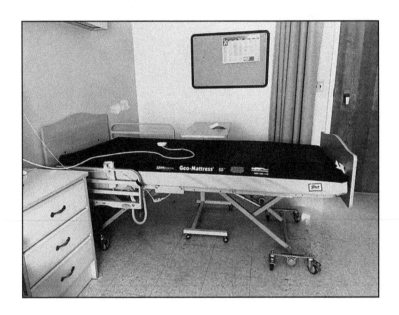

You mumbled for most of my visit in tongues and syntax I can't quite catch. It feels almost like English, but impossible to decipher. Pleas for forgiveness and anger poke their way through your mind scramble from time to time. I tell you I hear your apologies and that you are forgiven many times over. I tried to karaoke the Beatles with you, but that doesn't seem to work anymore. You don't even seem to notice one bit that music is being played.

I refill the snack drawer and update the message to the staff.

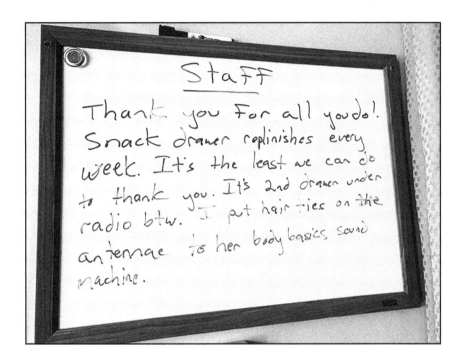

Staff

Thank you for all you do!. Snack drawer replinishes every week. It's the least we can do to thank you. It's 2nd drawer under radio btw. I put hair ties on the antennae to her body basics sound machine.

The poem I wrote on it months ago doesn't seem to apply anymore. It had said your mind waxes and wanes in secret rhythm with the stars. There doesn't seem to be any coming and going with your cognition anymore. It's just word salad. This makes it so hard to know if what I am doing has any impact. I try to keep a gentle hand on you through the medical gloves. I don't know if you feel it. You sometimes grab your companion stuffed cat or your own fingers to suck on like an infant might. You express extreme anger unpredictably and punch the rolling food table. A minute later you are crying and inconsolable. I can only make out 5% of what you are saying, so I have little aim upon which to shoot my soothing prayers.

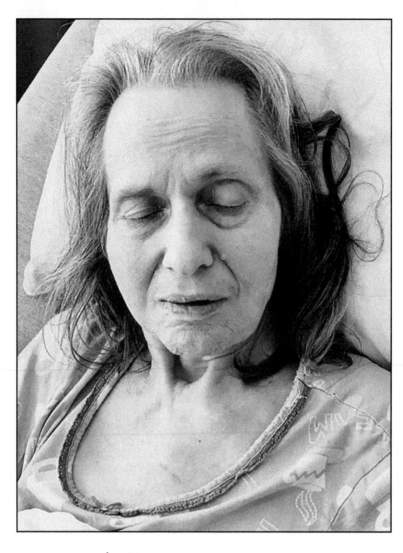

I pray anyway . . . in my own way.

A Post

L ast weekend my sisters visited you instead of me. I had a lot of work to do on the equinox so this was supposed to be a repose, but in many ways it felt even harder. Your hand and arm inexplicably were swollen and injured. Nobody seemed to know why. Tensions in our collective were high. Our empathy wails out in a collective cry.

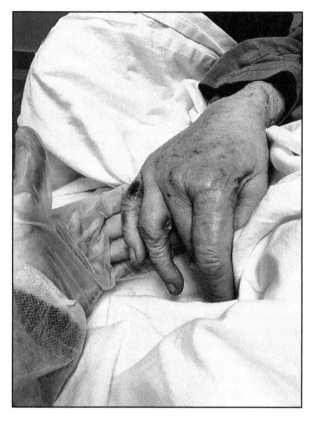

I will leave with a quote from a short story I am reading:

> I have heard it said that life is fragile and fleeting, but I don't believe it. It would be better if it was.

> *— Stephen King*

A Post

The new room was decorated interestingly on the neighbor's half. Though you can't really see, it inspired me to want to bring some art and stuffed animals for your half too. I will soon.

Your syntax was better this past weekend. I could make out some of what you wanted to say. It was mostly heartbreaking requests to get out. You feel trapped and useless. I assure you that your work on Earth continues, but I can completely empathize with what you are going through. It's a hardship few could bear with grace or equanimity. I try moving your stereo closer so The Beatles might capture you. They don't.

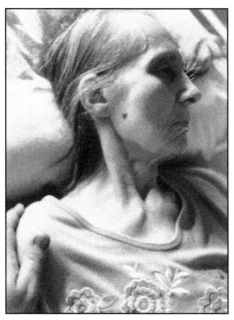

I leave more snacks in your drawer for the staff. The book I want to read to you came this week. I hope Ram Dass might get through to you. I don't feel like much is. You cry a lot in my presence. You beg for forgiveness. You beg for freedom. I try to remind you that your heart and higher self are always free, that you can still connect to that freedom in breath and meditation and music.

As I leave this week, I notice the beautiful woods across the street are being clear cut for probably another low rent college mega apartment complex. Seeing that pushes me over my limit. Now I am crying and feeling trapped too. If Narnia isn't safe, then nothing is.

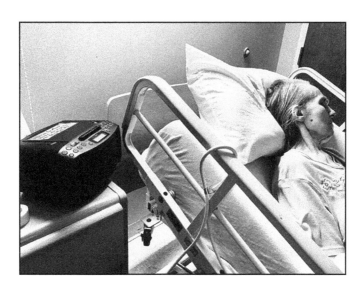

A Post

Today started with an innocent conversation from your roommate about pineapple in cottage cheese. It quickly devolved into you crying and complaining about being stuck while your roommate hurled racist insults at me and accused me of stealing. I was told that her son in law was going to beat the shit out of me if I had any shit left in me. I was told I wasn't raised up right and that I was a son of a b. I didn't take anything personally. This is aging. I know. I breathe. I definitely have empathy for the black staff though. I have never in all my life been called what I was called today. I won't repeat it here.

   We recited The Hail Mary and Our Father prayers several times. You remember them word for word. You say you talk to your mom now. That she doesn't love you. I insist we all love you. You apologize to your sister Mary and tell her you miss her. I feed you baked chips and ginger ale to try cheering you up. It works a little.

I ask how old you are. You say twenty something. As is tradition, Loretta joins us on video chat. We discuss getting you a new pillow better suited for your positions which never seem comfortable. We also discuss getting sippy-cups as you seem to fixate orally these days. By your bed, I hang up a painting by my friend Charles Richardson—"Cosmic Baby." I feel it might give some color even to your mostly blind eyes and be an appropriate metaphor for the path you are on.

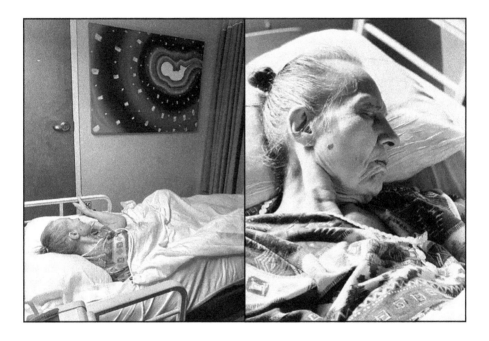

You come in and out of crying fits, but I don't leave until you have calmed down and are sleeping.

As you calm down, your roommate now asks me if I can open the window blinds. I oblige and the warm afternoon glow fills the room. The previously belligerent lady now offers me the warmest of smiles and gratitude for letting the sunshine in. I walk out quietly while you sleep and whisper "I love you."

A Post

Midweek thoughts: I don't know how you get through the long days. I feel we all just do our best to fill the hours and minutes with some purpose and happiness. How do you do that confined to a bed and blind and stricken with a myriad of medical conditions? Your hand and leg are now turning in and won't unfold. You will be sent to a neurologist. Could you have had a mini stroke? It's a mystery.

You're not eating much. At the behest of my sister, I emailed all the directors at your nursing home today asking about physical therapy. I missed the call from the physical therapist. I need to find time to call him back. That alone seems daunting. I ponder buying you really expensive sheets and making your bedroom fragrant with oils. How can anyone make you more comfortable at a time like this? Are you asleep while I write this? Do you sleep or hover in and out of consciousness never fully awake and never fully at peace? That space seems like territory you unfortunately might know all too well.

We spoke briefly today via whatsapp. I know you said something in response to me, but I can't remember how any of the conversation went. You seemed out of it. I look for something to hold onto, but it's all liquid and slips through my fingers before I have it. How could I do more? How could we as a people prepare better for this time of enduring and confusing transitions? Your every physical need has to be assisted or done by others now. They are all strangers, bless them, but strangers nonetheless. Strangers behind masks necessitated. Strangers who probably wipe the butts of hundreds of other strangers. Strangers who I desperately want to know and connect with, but feel impossibly separated by institutions, pandemics, responsibilities.

You are on a path most sacred, being held together by pillow sided mattresses and the care of strangers. And in this witnessing I am doing, I must acknowledge people are finding the kindest and gentlest ways to see me, to share with me, to acknowledge this experience. Maybe in some small way, your life now makes some of us less estranged from each other. There's a light in there somewhere. I am stumbling to find the words tonight to explain it. But it's there ... undying; flickering nonetheless.

I fell asleep cuddling your grandsons whose names and faces you can no longer recall. They don't know who you are either. A tear forms, and I slowly wake with the deepest of mind rattles seeping forward. I try to listen to the rattles. Is there music in it? Is it just keeping me awake? I turn on *The Office* and ask Jim, Pam, and Dwight to pacify me.

April 10, 2021

A Post

I sit here listening to the Beatles' "Across The Universe" interspersed with the neighbor's TV. It's enough to pay the exorbitant fees to allow you your own room, but "nothing's gonna change my world. Jai guru deva. om." I hang more art. I wipe down the walls. I put my newest haiku on the board. They were changing you when I got here. I cannot post the audio I took of that. It is just too heart wrenching to hear you cry and beg and scream in confused terror.

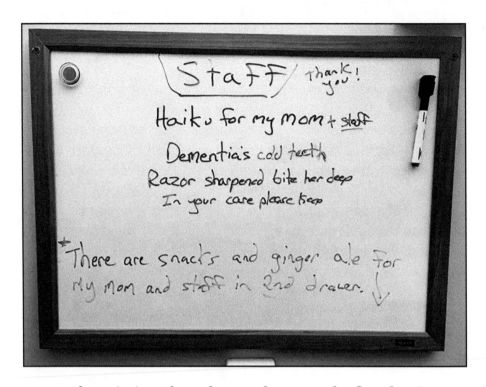

The painting I hung last week was on the floor leaning upside down. Thankfully the cosmic baby isn't damaged. I try securing it better, but I fear the tightness of your half the room will lead it to being bumped again. After your ordeal of being changed, you rock back and forth in a tight locked up position. You cry and say you don't understand why. I tell you I couldn't agree more. You fall asleep and stay that way. I sit here with you and totally alone.

> Dementia's cold teeth
> Razor sharpened bit her deep
> In your care please keep

> —Mark J DeMaio

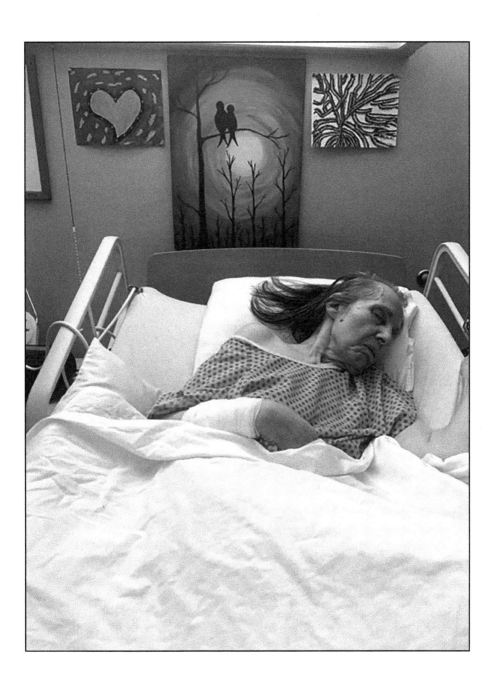

It occurred to me this week that you don't seem to know who I am anymore. But I trust showing up is enough because what else am I capable of doing other than showing up again and again. The feelings of futility in my witnessing caresses me into some tears. My mask catches them as "I, me, mine" bellows through your speakers. It switches to "Let It Be" and I pray the great mother is with you whispering words of wisdom. You feel beyond my reach. I pray for your release for both selfless and selfish reasons. "Let It Be" continues its mantra as I type and cry and just be here by your side.

A Post

My journey and yours feel too personal to share much anymore. Maybe that will change. You qualified for hospice. My emotions sometimes spill out in the ugliest ways. I was doing so well witnessing and holding space, but now I feel entitled and past due to some imaginary reward that my ego wrapped up over my inner sight. I write in the journal Loretta gifted me and let you sleep. This is our new normal.

I hung a few more things today—the beautiful flowers and crystal protection piece Loretta sent and the mystery rosary that has been following you around in your institutional journey.

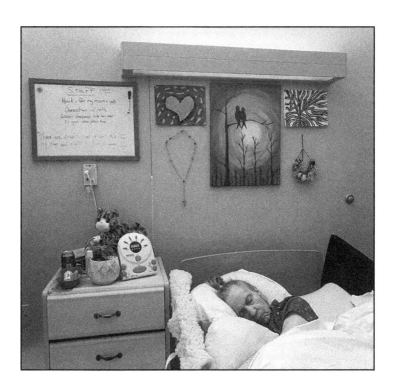

I try reading prayers, but they fall flat. I find talking about transformation, the indestructible nature of energy, matter, and consciousness to be far more meaningful. I order a book of zen poets who wrote pieces just before death.

Your speech is mostly garbled, but you manage to say that you don't want to die. I tell you only your skin is shedding. That there is no death. That you are riding on the wings of eternity like hyah hyah (thank you Saul Williams). I tell you that dementia is doing this to your body via your brain. You said you didn't know that. You hold my hand so tight. I have only felt that same intensity of grip from my wife during childbirth. Loretta says this is common in dementia patients, that there are methods to buffer it so you don't hurt your hand. I will bring a soft cloth to cover my hands on my next visit to protect you from further injury.

You cry. I cry. The CNA tells you to cheer up—that your son is here so you should be happy. This has happened a few times. I never know why they do that or what I should respond with. I don't need you to put on your best face as one CNA put it—I just want you to be exactly who you are and how you feel. So we feel deep universal thoughts and tears. We meditate on life and death and the purpose of a decaying body and mind.

A Post

A big part of making any communication effective is understanding how much anxiety there is in our world and recognizing how it manifests differently in each of us.

A Post

Your roommate yells at us to get out. She slams her remote against the table in perfectly aggressive dotted eighth notes. You spend most of our hours together mumbling sentences that have nouns and verbs but whose predicates get lost in the wash of dementia's spin cycle. You told me you knew who you were, but not who I was. I read you poetry about dying and you had something to say tearfully about every one. I had a hard time understanding any of the responses though. I wrote a new haiku for your board. We held hands. You are getting closer and closer to a fetal position—a sign of late stage dementia. I am distracted with my phone for much of our visit. I am emotionally checking out I guess. I will maybe turn it off next visit to help prevent that from happening again.

> Returning a child
> Lost in foggy forest deep
> Searching for new buds

—Mark J DeMaio

A Post

When I arrive, you are sleeping. Quickly you realize you have an audience and you allow yourself the tearworks of the deep true feels of your anxiety around all that's happening to you. I can't understand much of your words, but I assure you that I feel every bit of it. I tell you my wisdom teeth were pulled yesterday. You tell me it's unimportant. Interesting how that was so clearly stated. I ask you what important things I can tell you. You have no answer, so I start reminding you that death is just a word—a concept. And that reality isn't a word or a concept. I tell you that energy, matter, and consciousness can't die—that they merely swap shapes and forms in an eternal cosmic puzzle. Your roommate chimes in that I am full of bullshit. She throws a banana in my direction. I learn her name and ask Ms. Alice to please refrain from food fights. She screams for help. I ask you if you want me to get you a new roommate. You are non committal. You say something like you are both on the same road. I dunno. It's all garbled in dementia's fierce muzzle. But it feels like you aren't sure, so I won't request it yet.

Your dinner arrives and I feed you like I did when you first were hospitalized back in September. Only now the food has to be all mush for you to eat it. I remember back at the hospital when you tried to eat your napkin over and over again if I left you to your own devices. That's when I knew nothing would ever be the same.

And wow was I right.

The hospice social worker wants to know what my choice of crematorium is. I guess they want to know in case you go in the middle of the night and I am not awake to manage it. Hospice is available 24/7. It's a relief to have them. I also send them the dimensions of your columbarium that you will share with dad one day. Size, I didn't realize, is quite important in selecting an urn. If we were wealthy, we could fit your ashes into a big giant urn behind a big giant stone in some elaborate resting place. I saw those in New York when I was at Terri's (close friend) funeral. Keri (another close friend) is selling her house. You nod. Everything changes.

The roommate continues being belligerent. She screams for a spoon. We have an extra that I offer. She tells the CNA that I have diseases, and she hopes I die a horrible painful death. I laugh. What else is there to do Ms. Alice? I hope you both can find some humor and equanimity laying alone in a nursing home (featured recently on John Oliver I might add) being tended to by well intentioned but undertrained and underpaid and usually unaware staff. God I dread our roadmaps for the elderly. It's all of our roadmaps too. And this scenario is pretty privileged all things considered. And I ramble. I run my hands through your hair. I kiss you on your head and tell you I love you as visiting hours come to a close. I head outside not before admiring the courtyard we probably will never get to enjoy and the one extremely out of place painting which most definitely does not match the aesthetic. I walk outside and look to the wind to speak to and comfort me. The flag flaps in response just ahead of the palm tree shading my eyes from the scorching Florida sun.

A Message to My Siblings

She was sleeping when I got here. I really don't know what to report. I watched her sleep for three and a half hours. She definitely seems stable, but her hand is still making a claw and her body is curling up towards a fetal position. She opened her eyes once or twice, but never really woke up. I let her sleep.

A Post

Today you are asleep, and so I read while I sit vigil.

The ego is what experiences aging and death. It doesn't continue, but it is nearly impossible for the Ego to imagine its own demise. When the Ego thinks it's dying, it mistakes itself for the whole—body, Soul, and Awareness—and often people who are beginning to go through the long process of ripening into God run around to different doctors (and maybe even shrinks) because they develop an even more intense dread of death. Awareness, God, whatever you want to call it, is beyond time and concept. This is the Ground of Being.

—Ram Dass

Ripening into God! Ripening into God! Ripening into God!

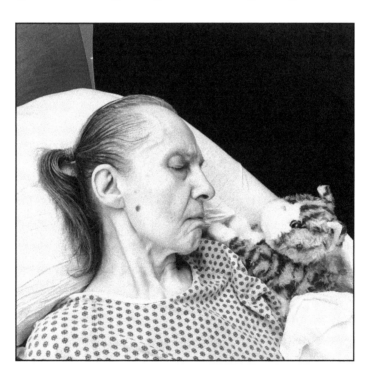

An Excerpt That I Forwarded to My Siblings

Honesty is reached by the doorway of grief and loss. Where we cannot go in our mind, our memory, or our body is where we cannot be straight with another, our world, or our self. The fear of loss, in one form or another, is the motivator behind all conscious and unconscious dishonesties: all of us are born to be afraid of loss, in all its forms, all of us, at times, are haunted or overwhelmed even by the possibility of a disappearance, and all of us therefore, are but one short step away from dishonesty. Every human being dwells intimately close to a door of revelation they are afraid to pass through. Honesty lies in understanding our close and necessary relationship with not wanting to hear the truth.

The ability to speak the truth is as much the ability to describe what it is like to stand in trepidation at this door, as it is to actually go through it and become that beautifully honest spiritual warrior, equal to all circumstances, we want to become. Honesty is not the revealing of some foundational truth that gives us power over life or another or even the self, but a robust incarnation into the unknown unfolding vulnerability of existence, where we acknowledge how powerless we feel, how little we actually know, how afraid we are of not knowing and how astonished we are by the generous measure of loss that is conferred upon even the most average life.

Honesty is grounded in humility and indeed in humiliation, and in admitting exactly where we are powerless. Honesty is not found in revealing the truth, but in understanding how deeply afraid of it we are. To become honest is in effect to become fully and robustly incarnated into powerlessness. Honesty allows us to live with not knowing. We do not know the full story, we do not know where we are in the story; we do not know who ultimately is at fault or who will carry the blame in the end. Honesty is not protection; honesty is not a weapon to keep loss and heartbreak at bay, honesty is the outer diagnostic of our ability to come to ground in reality, the hardest attainable ground of all, the place where we actually dwell, the living, breathing frontier where we are given no choice between gain or loss.

—David Whyte

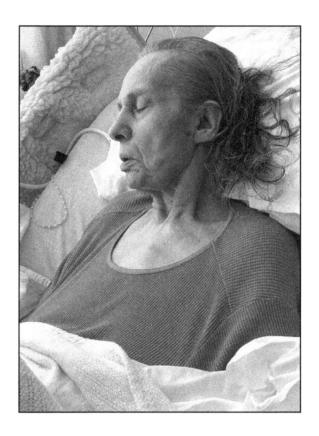

A Message to my Siblings

Here with mom. She had lunch. Now fast asleep.

An Update to My Profile Picture

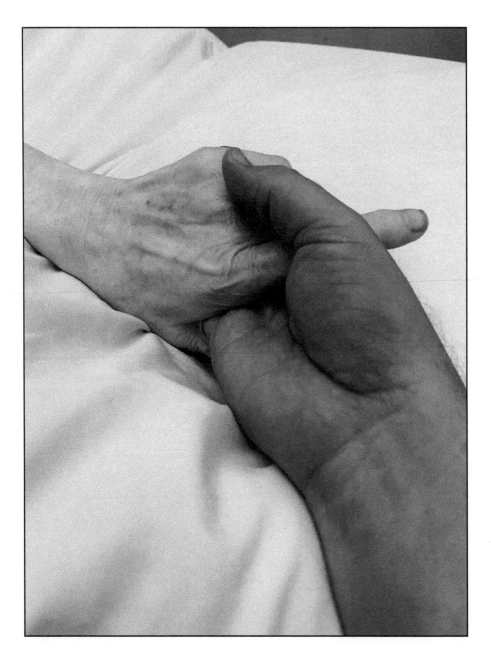

A Post

Your roommate relived a birth (and perhaps a rape) today. The baby she hallucinated was ten pounds and twelve ounces. She screamed bloody murder. I made a request for a new roommate. She has thrown one too many items of food at us for my liking. I fed you dinner. You said "I don't know," a lot. Not much else was comprehensible. I put a speaker bedside and we listened to hits from the 1950's. I rubbed oils on your arms and forehead and chest. I heard they are going to move you to room 132a. I hope they don't damage the painting again. At some point, someone put a thumbtack through it.

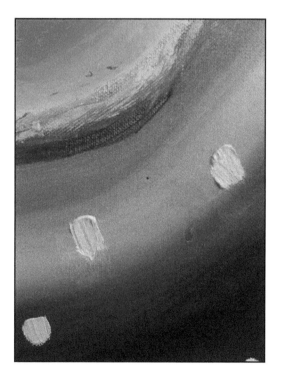

A Post

So tired of living in what feels like disfiguring pain all of the time. Keep hoping this too shall pass.

Note: This was posted while I was managing all of this for my mom and experiencing a lot of post surgical nerve pain that persisted.

Repost on Social Media

Someone once said when you love someone with dementia you lose them more and more everyday. When they are diagnosed, when they go through different stages, when they go into care and when they die. This is called "Ambiguous Loss". A Rapidly shrinking brain' is how doctors describe it. I wouldn't wish Dementia on anyone. As the person's brain slowly dies, they change physically and eventually forget who their loved ones are. They can eventually become bedridden, unable to move and unable to eat or drink.

A Post

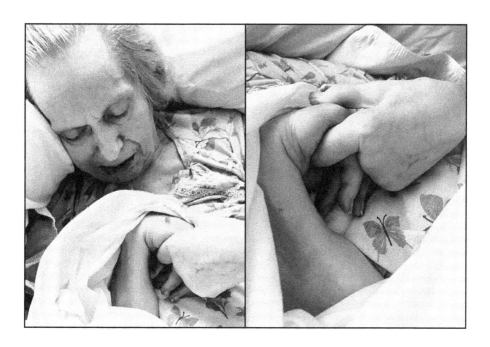

You are officially my sleepy weepy. Sleeping and weeping are really your only two past-times anymore. As you sleep hands locked together, I wonder if anyone has made music to die to. I know Mickey Hart made music to be born to. Maybe it's really the same thing and deserves the same music. I find a pretty album of ambient goodness titled "Music To Die To" by East Forest. We also listen to Red Shift Mantra.

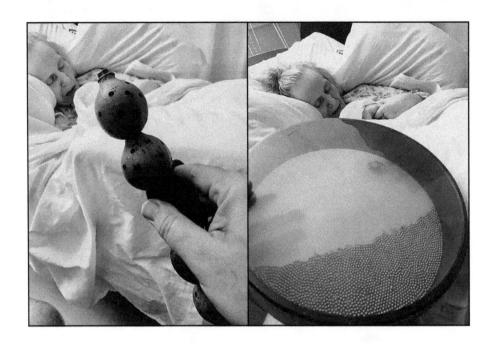

I play rattles and ocean drums and tap out rhythms on your curled up leg. I put essential oils on your head and chest and wrists.

I notice the oak tree out the window for the first time and imagine its aura extending out and over you. I visualize a beautiful extension of branches and leaves enveloping your space. I become impatient as the clouds outside draw dark and threatening and near—hoping you will suddenly have some epiphany and awake to the universal light. You don't stir.

You weep. No enlightenment suddenly strikes either of us. I continue to rattle and drum and offer to speak with you if you'd like to. You stay sleepy and weepy and don't say a word the whole two hours I am there. The CNA says this is your normal. I ask if you are reverse cycling and awake at night. She doesn't know, but doesn't think so.

I walk outside as visiting hours end and the air raps hard against my face. A strong wind keeps blowing. The trees sway in the knowing. And there's no comfort to be bestowing as we open ourselves to honest truth. At least not yet. Death isn't some quick moving epiphany that strikes like a bolt in the night. It's a marathon we pace ourselves to for a distance we cannot know or see or even imagine. You are reluctantly and slowly turning to death on your own sweet time and my aching heart wants you to be free now. Maybe that feeling is just about me and my wants. Our stuff is mixed and mingled by the cosmic chaos of the family matrix. I am bound to you, but feel lost in how to serve you best now. I keep rattling. I keep anointing. I keep tapping rhythms on your leg. I pray the oak tree will find you and hold you in it's loving rootedness.

May 31, 2021

Song Lyrics sent by a Friend

You will be free from the bonds that bind you
You are free from the bonds that bound you

— *Wardruna*

A Post

I notice there is some wetness and labor to your breathing today. You feel warm. The CNAs have no response or knowledge for my inquiries. The nurse on call lists some numbers off a sheet showing that everything is "fine." But it's not. I message hospice. They help escalate things. Meanwhile the AC isn't working in your room. I am on a mission to advocate for you tonight. The AC is being repaired. I am playing a temple bell to the Beautiful Chorus.

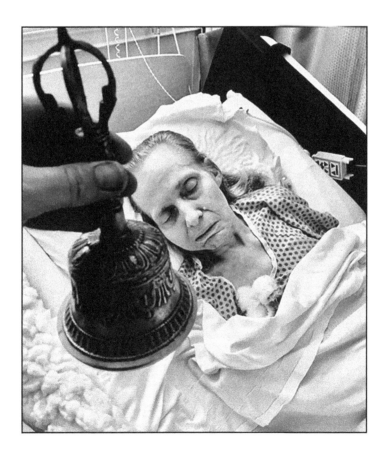

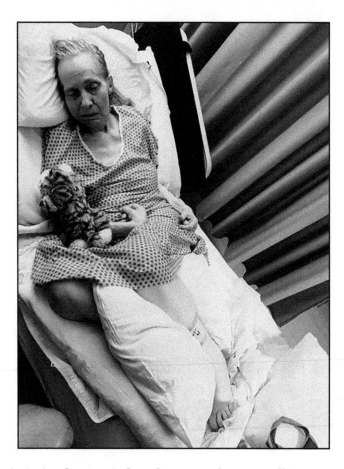

Your brain in its dementia has forgotten how to tell your mouth
to chew. You have aspirated on cheeked food. Your lungs sound
like my rattles. And so I don't leave your side at the end of visiting
hours. I sit and wait. Help arrives. On this journey there have been
many allies along the way. Taylor, the on call nurse with hospice,
is one of those tonight. I owe her a lot of gratitude. She made
everyone do their jobs and do right by you. She changed you and
dressed your wounds and told me hospice will be getting you moon
boots for your diabetic legs and feet. She took the time to explain
things to me that I didn't know. I expressed that I sometimes feel
insecure in how much I don't know. She made it ok for me to not
know. She did the knowing for us all. She probably doesn't realize
how much she helped me in walking you home tonight. I repeat to

you that I wish nothing more than to set you free though it is not in my power to do so. I repeat it often. I clean your companion cat with the evidence of your cheeked food laid out upon its own cheek.

I talk to your neighbor who keeps insisting her TV doesn't work although it's on the whole time. She calls for staff. She cry-laughs uncontrollably. It's unsettling. It's been four hours. I am here in my hunger and my thirst. My pains are nothing compared to yours. You finally seem comfortable, and so I wait. You sleep. Night creeps. I ponder the doctor's recommendation for comfort meds as the order for oxygen is sent up the line. Everything will be re-evaluated in the morning. You may get pneumonia. You may not make it out of these woods. I want nothing more than to set you free though it is not in my power to do so. I may be here all night.

Song Lyrics

Ah, because the world is round, it turns me on
Because the world is round, ah
Because the wind is high, it blows my mind
Because the wind is high, ah
Love is old, love is new
Love is all, love is you
Because the sky is blue, it makes me cry
Because the sky is blue, ah, ah, ah, ah

— The Beatles

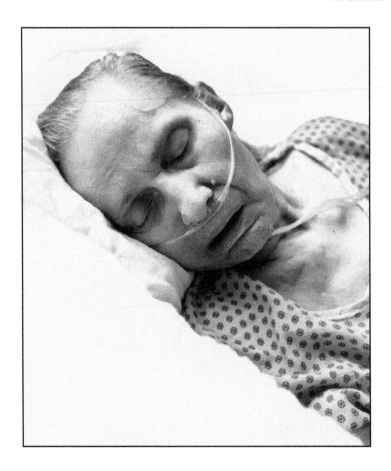

A Quote

When we cease to resist our grief, we learn that, painful though it may be, grief is an integral part of elder wisdom, a force that humbles and deepens our hearts, connects us to the grief of the world, and enables us to be of help.

—Ram Dass

Some Random Journal Entries While Sitting Vigil

Wind whipping wonder
Flags beat across their perches
A mother dying
*

Your breath's shallow wheeze
Only comfort for your needs
Morphine, oxygen
*

Join the ancestors
The priest forgave you all your trespasses
The nurse dropped the morphine under your tongue
There's nothing your mind can do to keep your body alive
What must it be like inside there?
Do you know who I am? Who you are?
Are you like a baby's consciousness scrambling to nothingness—
As we keep your body barely alive

—Mark J DeMaio

A Post Celebrating LGBTQ Month and My Mom

A little story about my mom and me: When I was in my 20's, I came out (in a manner of speaking) as not being Catholic. This was a big thing for me. I asked my mom if she would come to my wedding if it weren't in the Catholic Church. She was pretty adamant that no she would not because the marriage would be spiritually a sin if not sanctified at the church. Long story short—when I was married in my 30's outside at Birdsong Barn by a married couple of non-denominational reverends, she was there. I've got the photos to prove it.

People change. Tolerance grows. My mom, for all her small town Iowa Catholic guilt upbringing is beautiful proof. I wouldn't equate it to anyone else's journey, but I do leave it here to illustrate perhaps there is hope for growth and acceptance even in our older age. And come to think of it, myself being brought up so conservative middle class and Catholic, I never would have imagined that as an adult I would be doing a Kids Fringe workshop called Drums-n-Drag with Gidget Galore. But there I was. Thanks by the way Gidget. You were professional and fun to work with. I'm so glad we did it. That said, I suppose I've changed a lot too. All the best this month to the LGBTQ community. I hope acceptance and understanding and compassion just keeps on growing in this mixed up world we find ourselves in.

June 3, 2021

A Post

Father Benjamin Lehnertz performed the sacrament Anointing of the Sick on my mom yesterday. I assisted and was able to fall right back into the Catholic rituals (which I actually find have some meaning and beauty when they are looked at with the right set of eyes). He was kind, sweet, and humble. His prayer book was tattered and even his sash looked like a Weasley family hand me down. It was a special spiritual moment regardless of religion or belief. I will cherish that memory for a long time—especially him greeting an elderly Spanish speaking woman in the hallway with his innocent and awkward "Soy Padre Ben-ha-min."

A Post

Holding you in the light. So grateful for your roommate's family agreeing to a temporary move so we could have the room to ourselves. I opened the curtains, I turned up the music. And most importantly, I turned off your roommate's TV immediately.

A Post

Is today the day you die? Can I find your soul in this cosmic sea of endless rubbish? Will you find mine? I've been so composed all day and then the tears hit me like a sucker punch. Where did they come from? I, your death doula, listen to the bated electronic breathing of this damn oxygen machine for hours on end. Our egos clashed some in this lifetime. I hope your soul will alight to mine. I hope our ancestors heal with us. I am sitting vigil today with that intention.

A Post

The first djembe I ever owned is bedside with you. I was able to sleep here last night. I drummed a bit. Your BP was 75/31 just an hour ago. Quartz and obsidian are laid out with intentions upon your steady but shallow breathing chest. I awoke before sunrise and opened all the shades expecting this could be your last sunrise as Patricia Ann DeMaio. We listen to The White Album, and I tap the djembe. Strangers keep coming in to pay respects. My compassion for the staff grows. For better or worse, what a job this must be! Some can't help but immediately divulge their families' experiences around aging and the inevitable dramas that ensue. I pray for a quick and peaceful release. We wait.

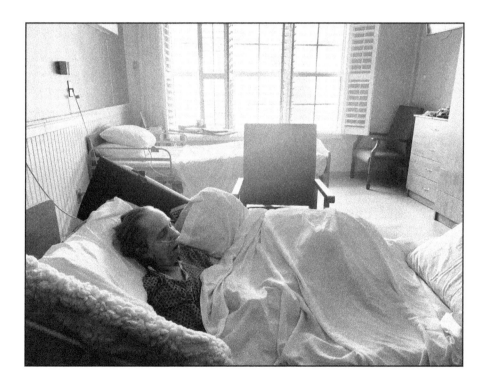

A Memory

I returned from having dinner at my home to find you alone and breathing very laboriously. I am confused by the new patterns. It's interesting how quickly we adapt to new norms and just expect them to continue. I had grown accustomed to the patterns of your breath and the oxygen machine. Now something is different, off. I call on my friend who knows a lot about death and physiology. Interestingly enough, instead of focusing on my questions about your new symptoms, she starts going down a checklist of what is spiritually appropriate to assist with the dying. She notices I have hit every item on the checklist, but then asks me if I have read you *A Prayer for the Dead* by Byron Ballard. She suggests I ask the nurse to get your morphine to you a bit early so you don't experience unnecessary pain, and that I read the poem. As I return with the nurse, I begin to hear your death rattles. The nurse seems more confused than I do. I ask the nurse if you are still with us. She says she doesn't know and needs to get a supervisor. She scurries off. I'm left alone with you. A Prayer for the Dead pings my phone at that very moment. I start reading it over you as tears pour out of me uncontrollably. I have no idea what I'm reading. I'm heaving. I'm being torn apart, but I feel so clearly the power in the words I'm reading. The fog of my grief keeps me from mentally understanding what I'm saying, but it feels like a powerful incantation I must see through to completion. I carry on and push the prayer out.

An Incantation Right At Death

A Prayer for the Dead
You have come to the end of this pathway
In a journey to which we bear witness.
You have come to the end of a pathway
That is barred with a gate and a door.

May this door open swiftly and silently.
May this gate give you a moment's grace
In which to rest your spirit before you venture through.
We stand here with you, as your companions,
As your family, for you are beloved.
But, for now, we must remain here.
We can not go with you to this old land.
Not yet.

For you will see the Ancestors.
You will see the Beloved Dead.
You will walk among the Divine Beings
That guide and nurture us all.
You go to dwell in the lands
Of summer and of apples
where we dance
forever youthful, forever free.
We can hear the music in the mist
The drums that echo our sad hearts.
We can see your bright eyes and your smile.
And so we open the gate.
We push back the door.
We hold the gate open.
We glance through the doorway,
And with love and grief and wonder
We watch you walk through.
Hail the Traveler!
All those remembered in love, in honor,
Live on.
Farewell, o best loved,
O fairest,
Farewell

—Byron Ballard

Late Night/Early Morning — A Post

Your corpse lay beautifully serene before me. I place the wreath of protection, your rosary, and your stuffed cat with you in the bed.

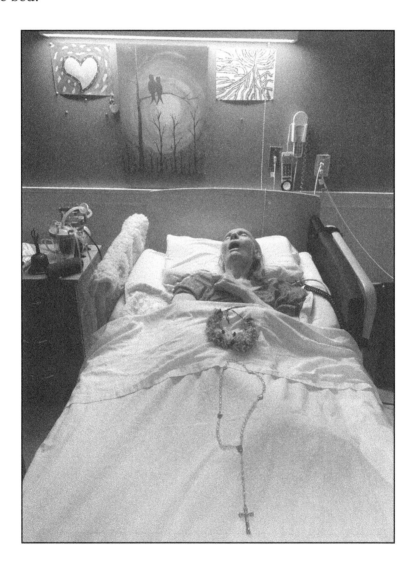

I recite a prayer for the dead over you as I weep your gown wet. My mind finds the most pointless regrets and my tears wash away the guilt of things I know I shouldn't feel guilty for. But the mind. It races. I am alone for a few minutes with you as the nurse gets a supervisor. I heave uncontrollably. I welcome the suffering of my grief as yours is now eternally allayed. I am both completely at peace and fully grieving. My sister arrives. We embrace. We hold for a few minutes as the CNAs bathe your corpse. I am so grateful three of my sons got to say goodbye today. I am so grateful for so much. We return to the room. You look angelic frozen in time. My wife arrives. I play my djembe at your feet. We listen to other beautiful music and embrace each other. I thank you for being so considerate even in death. You waited for every one of your children to visit. You waited until my school year was over. You even waited for me to return to you tonight after I left you alone with my brother earlier. I am so grateful you waited for me. I am so grateful it was me with you when death came. I knew it would rip me open, but I welcomed it because it meant I got to open that gate for you. I got to walk you home. There's no greater honor anyone could have bestowed on me. I am forever blessed by my journey with you in your aging and suffering. I cry. The room cries. We stand frozen in time over your motionless glowing body.

And then . . . .

I smell smoke. Nah. I must be imagining things. My nose is all clogged from crying. My wife doesn't smell it. Moments later my brother in law texts that the fire department is here and there is smoke everywhere and they may be evacuating the building. It all takes me back to one of our family's defining moments: a house fire of April 18, 1988 at 28 Willowbrook Road. And so here we are.

Our cars are blocked in. Firemen are on the roof. The gurney to the funeral home must sneak you out the back door. I wear your rosary and later will add it to the ancestor altar. Bravo mom. Great show.

Hail the traveler!

A Post

It's very hard. I am very sad deep in my bones. I cry without warning. I welcome it all though. This is the way.

Hail the Traveler!

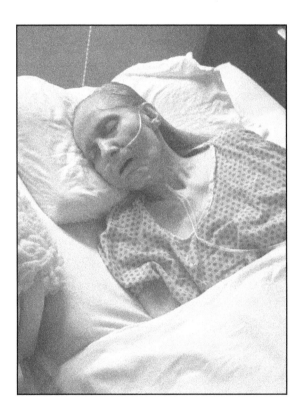

A Post

My reflections, I realized, aren't over. I helped open that gate, but I had to stay here. And since the beginning of September, as hard as it's always been, caring for you has been so much of my life. And so much I wanted for your release from suffering, so much I wanted to walk you home in peace and love, but there's so much more for me to tell on this journey that yet again I struggle to find the words to express. I don't know if there is a stage of grief called 'void,' but that's where I am at. The void. I don't want to do or not do anything. Both seem comparably like purgatory. You were so much of my life these last months that I don't know what's left to look forward to.

My visits, for all their challenge of spirit and compassion, had become such a big part of my life that I'm left now not knowing how to fill the giant space that remains where I put you in my heart week after week. Every shower washes something away, and I add my tears to the drain. I know this too must be part of the process—this listless empty feeling in me. Crying is preferable. I try to welcome this void like a guest because I know this is part of my healing, but it's just such a damn annoying houseguest. I drum. I walk. I play tennis. I try to move the energy in my body. It helps, but damn the day has just so many freaking hours to it.

I use up what points are left on your Discover card to get you an urn. It's really quite beautiful. I decide we'll do your service on your birthday, August 28th, because that will mark exactly one year since there was probably a UTI beginning to rage within you that would exacerbate your dementia and never let you return to your previous baseline. It seems fitting. I notice ibis and zebra long wings on my walk. Dad always spoke to us through dragonflies. Are one of these your new calling card? It's hard to say as the inspiration to feel into things is flatlined.

I go through the motions like I know I should. I remember a friend who used to sign her emails with the following: "If you are going through hell, keep going."

I'll keep going.

A Retrospective

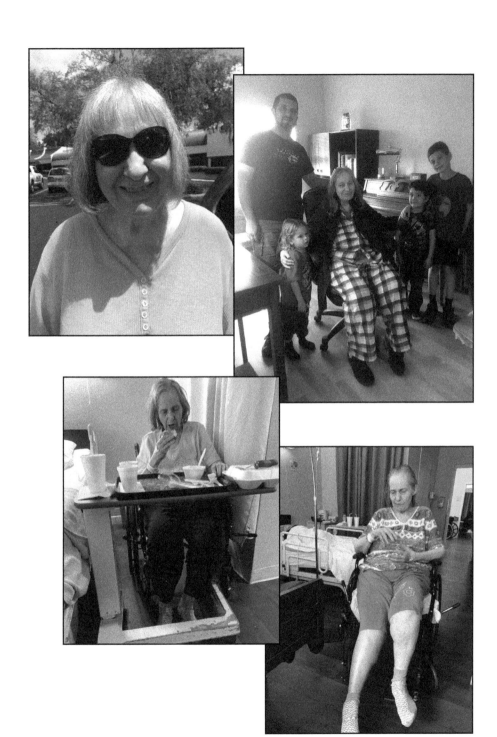

A Post

The void in me is your legacy. Not that you would have wished for this deep persistent heartache, but there it is. And it nonetheless must burn its purifying way to completion. No false strength.

A Quote

Grief can destroy you or focus you. You can decide a relationship was all for nothing if it had to end in death, and you alone. OR you can realize that every moment of it had more meaning than you dared to recognize at the time, so much meaning it scared you, so you just lived, just took for granted the love and laughter of each day, and didn't allow yourself to consider the sacredness of it. But when it's over and you're alone, you begin to see that it wasn't just a movie and a dinner together, not just watching sunsets together, not just scrubbing a floor or washing dishes together or worrying over a high electric bill. It was everything, it was the why of life, every event and precious moment of it. The answer to the mystery of existence is the love you shared sometimes so imperfectly, and when the loss wakes you to the deeper beauty of it, to the sanctity of it, you can't get off your knees for a long time, you're driven to your knees not by the weight of the loss but by gratitude for what preceded the loss. And the ache is always there, but one day not the emptiness, because to nurture the emptiness, to take solace in it, is to disrespect the gift of life.

—Dean Koontz, Odd Hours

A Post

I wanted to grieve longer. I was expecting I would. I wanted to let it envelop me like an old blanket. I wanted to explore the depths of my grief with honesty and intention. But rapidly the responsibilities of money and the family flooded my consciousness, and I am back to managing things full tilt. I feel cheated, though I know this all needs to be done—though I know I agreed to it. Maybe it's that. Maybe it's that I allowed myself to feel so much in the months leading up to now that it all poured out of me at the event horizon. Maybe. Maybe grief will revisit me later. Hail the traveler. Godspeed my sweet mama.

A Post

My dad would have been 95 today. To honor his day, I collected my mom's ashes from the funeral home. It was not planned, but it just happened that way. Synchronicity or what have you. On her birthday on August 28th, her remains will rejoin him at the columbarium at Queen Of Peace in Gainesville. Time represents rhythms and seasons. And so we honor their seasons in marked out rhythms of significant time. And so it is. Happy birthdays. Happy transitions. Happy returns. Hail the travelers.

A Post

Today's grief is a slow burn. It can't seem to fully boil into fruition, nor can it allow me the comfort to just fall asleep. I lay awake imagining all those months all you could do was be in bed. It makes my bed feel like a prison for a moment. The mind scrambles for justifications of why I had to put you in the nursing home. And they are all valid, but I hurt at the loneliness of a nursing home bed during covid to a blind woman with dementia. It seems like yesterday I was dreaming of getting us a wheelchair accessible van and taking you on riverside walks at Blanchard Park while the sounds of my kids playing nearby would serenade you to the hue of earth's glorious waterside sunsets. I imagined you growing older with grace as covid restrictions were lifted. But you had done that already, hadn't you? You didn't come full circle back into my life to age. You came to me to die. One of my best memories of the 9 months I walked you home is singing the Beatles together. We'd have a small moment of shine like that. I'd try clinging to it —recreating it on the next visit. But it never was to be. Your decline was so fast and furious. There was so much you needed to let go of. And now, in your physical absence, I find myself needing to let go of so much. I picked up your ashes on dad's birthday. Uncle Duane died that very same day. What's the cosmic connection? The mathematical improbability of it all seems to tell a story written in a language I can't decipher. There's no Rosetta stone for the soul. I dropped a thank you card off the other week for the family of your roommate at the time of your death. They were so kind to let me stay vigil with you all night. While dropping it off, a middle aged son was talking to someone in the activities' department. He was saying he was going to visit every single day. I felt like the old experienced pessimist next to this energetic first timer. I stayed silent in my jealousy that this new family would be able to visit every day now. That simply wasn't the case as we set all this up at the height of the pandemic. I muse that the restrictions in place may have saved my family here in Orlando

100

from losing me entirely in my service to you? Would I have bitten off more than I could chew? Would I have been by your side every day? It's very possible that I would have. And so I push back the feelings that I could have done more, that I should have done more. I have to be gentle with myself. I had no roadmaps. I had no mentor in this death doula business. I have to be gentle, but sometimes it's so hard to pacify the remorse of time lost, touches not fully given, etc etc. I wish I could drive that short little journey to your miserable prison bed and touch you one more time, to tell you how much I loved you in this life and will continue to love you in the next.

A Post

It is so much easier for man to act and re-act than it is for him to not-act. The Taoists refer to the art of "non-action" as Wu-Wei. It does not mean sitting idly by, but rather being patient, learning to see beyond our physical and emotional re-actions so that we may become more mindful in the moments when there is nothing to do but act. In my opinion, any action that exists for no-purpose other than the enjoyment of itself is a form of moving meditation Wu-Wei. Music, Dance, Art, Yoga, etc. The bird does not sing for the advancement of music. The cat does not stretch to post a selfie. The Whooping crane does not leap to have an article in National Geographic. If we play just to play—if we dance just to dance—we are not sitting idly by, but are mingling with Wu-Wei. We have stepped out of our normal day to day consciousness and are inadvertently connecting to the divine within ourselves. The way to do this is simply to find play for the purpose of play—to seek moments simply for your own personal enjoyment. When the mind has no desire to please, hurt, impress, manipulate, or influence any other person—it becomes free to connect directly to the emotional body, to the collective unconscious, to the higher self.

A Post

It's been a month already. Hard to believe. Something I hope people will take from my experience is that dementia is a terminal disorder. It's right in black and white on your death certificate. I think we have a tendency to gloss it over with the humorous image of an old person forgetting things. But things keep disappearing for someone with dementia. Memories. Skills. The decline to complete memory loss is different for each patient, but that's the event horizon for the diagnosis. Eventually the mind forgets how to talk entirely. It then forgets how to eat and drink. Eventually it simply forgets at all how to tell the body to survive and so the dementia patient curls up into a fetal position as the body shuts down non-necessary functions in a last plea for its own survival. But the dementia brain offers no quarter and death awaits. And this is a completely natural thing. We made my mom's journey as peaceful and beautiful as we could. Her death, though mourned because she was loved, is not a sad event in the course of things. It's a powerful and beautiful and liberating event that also involves a lot of grieving because that's what love brings up for the purpose of healing. And here I am still grieving, but in all sorts of weird micro-sorrow moments that only seem to have a few breaths to call their own. My mom's children need me. My children need me. The community hopefully still wants what I have to offer. So I get back to the grind and try to find her inside of a quiet moment now and again. I am working on a book. I hope it will help others. Good night World.

A Reflection Journal: What now?

As I pass the month milestone of my mother's transition, I find myself thinking this story needs a bit more. Looking at it as a whole, it definitely had its defining conflict which led to a most dramatic climax and spoke to me on the soul level of existence. I hope in describing the terrain of ripening up to God, I may have made a small dent in the collective fabric—a dent of compassion and connection, of honesty and witnessing. I saw so many on this journey clinging to and holding on to what was, not giving their loved ones the freedom and strength and honesty to celebrate what comes next. I read recently that in some cultures, they never hang up pictures of the family of the loved one when they know they are dying. Instead, at the foot of the bed, they place beautiful paintings of what artists envision the afterlife to be like. They encourage the loved one to celebrate and look forward to their transition the way many of us look forward to a birth. One transition begets another. It's how the universe works. Looking back, could it be a synchronicity that I intuitively hung "Cosmic Baby" beside her all those months when she was at her most progressed.

I also read that Tibetan Masters will sit up, take three extraordinary long breaths, and then die. I find it heart pounding to reflect that I had moved my mother's bed into a more upright position due to the changes in her breathing. Shortly after, she took several prolonged breaths and then died. How did she know? She died a masterful death. Did she also show me the power of consciousness beyond the physical by messing with some electrical wires and starting a small fire on her journey from this state to the next? It sure does seem like anything is possible. My work on her behalf is far from over. I've taken over so many roles for the family to which I feel thrust into and stressed out by but somehow perfectly qualified for. That's a story for another time though. There's a vast world of logistics and work in being responsible for a family. These logistics are important to handle with grace and a calm head. It's important to do estate and family planning. It's so vitally important.

This moment in time is a struggle personally. I think any reader should be aware that post-transition-depression is normal. I call it my GFD: generalized funk disorder. While death is associated with sadness, being around that level of the soul's work is also a sort of spiritual high. You mourn with your senses so jacked and the poignancy of every moment so apt. It's not sustainable in the least. I know I mentioned feeling cheated of that time in the heightened awareness triggered by my mom's transition. It wasn't able to last long. It, like life, is transient. The come-down from that grieving death high can be very hard. It's where I am at now. Life seems so tragically normal and uneventful. I am trudging physically and emotionally through my days. I'm bored. Being in service to my mom was a gift. Now I feel giftless. And so....

What comes next for me? In regards to the topic of the dying process, I'm planning on enrolling in a workshop on Conscious Living and Conscious Dying. I intend to further my witnessing at the soul level via volunteering or perhaps as a death doula. I don't have a timetable set for all of this, but I'm committed to doing it. There's something profoundly alive about being fully present with someone dying. I want to make that a part of my life and spiritual work now that it has touched me so profoundly.

I also wanted to let the World know the last words my mom spoke to me. It was the Tuesday that I went in for my regular visit on the evening of June 1st. It became apparent something was off. I later found out she was starting the 'transitioning' or 'active dying' stages which would run to completion on June 4th at 8:38 pm. She turned to me as I held her hand and stroked her hair. She barely could get the sounds out, but she did. She said it to me then as clearly as anything I had heard in months from her. I hope her words carry on the way she has.

I LOVE YOU

104

A Letter to My Children

Dear Kids, when I die, I hope you will fight over your inheritance. I hope there will be a great passionate ignition of soul sparks as you decide who gets the most treasured of my loot. I sure as hell hope this argument won't be about my bank account or my car or the silver coins at the ancestor altar.

I really hope you'll each want my cast iron pans. How many thousands of meals have I made you in them? How many beads of sweat have merged with oils and seasonings in this timeless nurturing ritual?

I also hope you'll want my notebooks. I hope you will pour through every page struggling to decipher my handwriting but hoping to know me better. I hope you will find the humanity and love in my flaws and vulnerabilities. How much have I said to the page trying to make sense of what goes on in my head?

I hope there will be a great gnashing of teeth to lay claim to my drums...which I have played millions of notes selflessly for thousands of ears in hopes that my intentions may somehow vibrate more drops of love to the cosmic seas. I hope the sounds the drums make will forever be a comforting reminder of me.

I hope you'll argue over what true wealth is in an honorable and honest way. I hope you'll find comfort in sharing what we can with each other in these fast and fleeting days, and I really hope every shared meal cooked in my cast iron pans will heal you. And I hope every mystery revealed of my hopes will bend your minds ever so slightly to a greater understanding of how the beat of my heart drummed for you. When I was tired. When I was lonely. When I wanted to quit. My heart kept drumming for you.

Love,

Papa

A Story About Mark's Jamaican Restaurant

Sometimes a place sticks on you like superglue whether you intend it or not. For me, Mark's Jamaican is one of these places. My wife and I like to drive a few minutes up the road to escape our home from time to time. One time, it was the evening Biden and Harris accepted the nomination for the executive branch. We listened in awe at the understandable frustration from the owners and friends at the restaurant as the introduction of Kamala completely left out any mention of her Jamaican heritage. The introductions talked heavily of her Indian bloodline though. Those in the establishment felt justifiably omitted from her history. I really got it in my bones that night. I felt so sorry for much of history's befuddling omissions, but especially the one happening in real time right before our eyes and ears on the TV screen. Trump still had not even conceded and a January 6th loomed just a few months around the corner. I silently prayed Kamala would make these people proud. I still do.

While my mom was in nursing care, I would pick up Mark's takeout from time to time. One time, I ran into some CNAs from the nursing home. We struck up a conversation. I asked if they were more fans of the curry or the jerk. We talked about spice preference and heat tolerances. I asked how they liked the company they worked for, and if they thought it was a good place to put a loved one. I talked about my mom. They said they knew her. They told me she was so sweet, and they loved doting on her. I of course picked up their tab that night. It felt like a cosmic opportunity to ensure some guardian angels in my mom's corner. The hostess who witnessed the whole thing said she was about to cry.

Months later my mom was in the active dying stages. I had just spent 6 to 7 hours by her side learning she was unlikely to make it through the week. It was the evening of June 1, 2021. I didn't want to leave her that night, but the nursing home would not let me stay. I gave my information to the head night nurse and asked her to please call me anytime if my mom's

106

condition changed. I was distraught. I was also really hungry and just needed a nurturing meal. I imagined myself devouring a vegetarian jerk dish with extra garlic from Mark's. It's one of my favorites. The aromatics alone inspire quite a fascination in me. Anyway, being around death is like this sometimes. You come away from it needing to affirm your own conviction for living. Eating is like that.

I looked up Mark's and it said I had 30 minutes before closing. I called ahead. No answer. I called ahead again. No answer. I drove over quickly to see them locking the door just after 9 pm. A man was at the door. I didn't know if he was an employee or a friend of the owner. He saw the look of frustration on my face. I asked if they were really closed because I just really needed a good meal and nothing else around was open except for a subpar chain sub shop a few doors down. The woman behind the counter chimed in that the kitchen had closed because they were slow. I have worked in the service industry and could empathize, but I'm sure they could see the lost look on my face as it just seemed one more punch in the cosmic gut. I asked if there was any food at all I could pay for. She said no. The man, however, asked me what was going on and what I was going to order. I told him that I had been bedside watching my mom die, and I didn't know how much longer she had to live. I told him I was craving a veggie jerk platter. I told him I just needed sustenance, and I wasn't ready to put on my father-suit and head home to my family yet. I told him I just needed a quiet moment to eat and process what was happening to my mom, to me, to my family. He looked at me in what I perceived as compassion and gently asked me if I liked oxtail and goat. I said that I absolutely love oxtail and goat. He told me to wait a minute.

Moments later I was walking to my car with a to-go bag of the lunch he would have to replace on June 2nd. He wouldn't take a penny from me. He handed me the bag and insisted I enjoy it in peace. He sent me on my way. I returned to Mark's the next evening to order the veggie platter, to offer my deepest gratitude to whoever the man was, and to leave a nice tip for whoever was there. I never have thanked him in person. I still don't know who he was. But the other night I was back at Mark's and reminded of all this history I have there. I just wanted to take a page in my book to thank that man, to thank Mark's for being a space where this kind of thing happens, and for making a damn fine life-affirming meal time and time again.

Addendum 1

Aunt Mary's Stories

My mom's sister was unable to visit during this time as she was experiencing her own journey with her husband Dwayne. In lieu of that connection, she did send some stories, and I want to honor them with their own space.

Story 1:

Pat, this note is from your sister, Mary. Do you remember when you were almost 16 and I was 12? We were at Leach Lake in northern Minnesota. Paul, a handsome and nice, 17 year old was interested in you, and you had a bit of a crush on him. I tried to get you out of our cottage, and we got into a bit of a fight as I tried to drag you out. Paul and parents had to leave, and your crush persisted. He did like you. Do you remember the teenage Ojibwa Indians who spotted you and me sitting in the car. They sat on the bumper and rocked the car until our parents returned. We also visited Itasca State Park where there was the claim that this little stream that I jumped across was the origin of the Mississippi River.

Story 2:

When you were close to 20 and I was a mature 16, we spent two weeks in a lovely cottage on Lake Okoboji. About 5 am I woke up and went to the living room to see what was causing a terrific roaring. A tornado was passing nearby. The picture window looked as if the lake was trying to come in. You slept through all the noise. Okoboji had Arnold's Park where there were fun rides and miniature golf. We played a lot of miniature golf. I couldn't get you to go to the indoor roller skating rink. If you had come, I would have had dates for us with two college sophomores. They thought I was in college too though I told them otherwise. They did not believe me when I said I was in high school. Remember the ride in the paddlewheel boat with the aspiring beauty queens who were contending for Miss Iowa. You and I walked a lot along the lake to Arnold's Park. This one day we were in a large, whirling ride that had no seats. My pedal pushers split on the inside of one leg. The college guys were eyeballing us, but I had to change my pants.

You helped me maintain my modesty as we walked back to our cottage on this beautiful, tree lined walk with the lake on one side and private lake homes on the other side. Though I roller skated with one of the college fellows for over an hour, we never got together again even though they did keep eyeballing us later.

Story 3:

Remember Yellowstone Park? Bobbie (oldest sister who died young) came with us on the long drive. You were almost 17. Mother got altitude sickness in the foothills of the Rockies. So we had to leave a cottage we were just about to rent and go to a lower altitude. By the time we got to Yellowstone, she had adjusted. Remember Old Faithful and the hot paint pots. Bobbie and I went on a three hour trail ride. It was just as well that you did not go because the horses had only recently been brought in from their winter range and did not appreciate riders. That night following the ride you stayed in the log cabin with me while I slept. Bobbie went with our folks to the main lodge. She talked with a mountain sheepherder and asked if it were true about herders who, deprived of human women, found female sheep handy. The answer: "Yes." Bobbie could get people to open up to her. Later that night there was a commotion outside as one of the log cabin renters encountered a bear as she was walking to the communal bathrooms. We did see a lot of bears asking for handouts.

Story 4:

James O'Malley!! We were both in high school at St.Pats. One day handsome, black haired James O'Malley walked me home from school. Pitter-patter went my heart until he started asking questions about you. Okay, I thought maybe he would ask you out. You weren't ready. Still and all, a lot of good looking fellows were interested in you.

Story 5:

Did your mother tell you that your grandmother Wall almost wasn't a Wall? Anita Pfeiffer's high school sweetheart and she were going to elope. He put a ladder against the house and was climbing it when your great grandfather, Mayor Frank Pfeiffer, caught him. Years later your grandmother was glad she did not marry the alcoholic sweetheart.

Story 6:

I've been thinking of stories about your mother. Pat was delayed in starting school because of what the doctors thought was a mild case of polio. When she did start school, she was shy and withdrawn--a natural target for bullies. The bullying ended when Bobbie found out about it. Bobbie beat up the bullies. Unfortunately for Bobbie, she was caught on the school grounds pounding on one of the bully boys as she sat on him. Your grandmother defended Bobbie to the nuns.

Story 7:

Pat was an avid reader and would read to me. Well. I was anxious to learn to read. So Pat taught me. This was during a time when educators thought all students should learn in lockstep. One of our favorite activities was walking the few blocks to the library once a week.

Story X:

I'm thinking of Pat on her birthday and the day of services
for her. Yearly, we would go to Durand, WI, our mother's
hometown. Her sister with husband, Bud VanDyke, and six
children lived in mother's old family home. The home had
been a showplace in its time. There was a second floor summer
sleeping porch. Pat was a couple of months from her ninth
birthday. Six of us kids had to sleep in a row on less than
comfortable mattresses. Of course, there wasn't much sleeping.
Terrell, the oldest Van Dyke daughter, had the baby sitting
duties while our parents were out socializing. Around midnight
we younger ones realized Terri had gone to sleep in her
bedroom. So we all went downstairs to discover Greg, maybe
11 or 12 years old, was having some whiskey. I was just five and
wide eyed, and I can still clearly see the events.

Addendum 2

An ongoing connection post

Something to note about chronic pain is scalability. When you are living with something for so long, it starts to become so utterly difficult to know if it is at all or ever improving. How do you scale it anymore? It's always there. Is it getting better? Are you just becoming more acclimated? Now when it gets really bad, then you know it got worse. Maybe in pain management, one must learn to celebrate perceived improvements even if it feels impossible to know for sure if there's anything to it. I mean, I know my pain feels way better now than when I had covid. But is it back to the baseline from before then? Has it gotten any better in the last two months? I have no idea. Scalability is just an internal filter that has no exact data associated with it. Did one of the kids do something infuriating? Did I lose a big contract? Did I just make love to my divinely beautiful wife? Did I just win the lotto? All of these things might affect my pain scores the moment I assess them. But has the pain really changed? I start to wonder about cells themselves. I mean, we know the body completely replaces the cells every 7 to 10 years or thereabouts. And though my musing mind might not recite straight science here, I wonder why these new cells recreate our scars and imperfections. Memory. Somehow they imprint memories from one generation of cells to the next. And is that what my pain is? A memory relay? If I could just forget it somehow. If I could just hypnotize myself? If I could just rewire things a bit so my memory loops stop feeding the vicious circle of pain, maybe then it would get better faster. Today, btw, is a good day. I feel like the pain is quite manageable. I woke up at 2:30am however aware of

113

it and the tinnitus. I fell to sleep so easily at 10:30 last night, but falling back asleep has proven futile. The words scalability and pain as an inherited memory start rolling around my skull, and before you know it I feel like I'll never sleep again unless I say something about it. I'm optimistic over time I can change my inherited memories. I'm optimistic today that I won't feel the pain in my head forever. And then I just chuckle and remind myself that I'm 44 and not getting any younger. Cramp in foot and ankle? Check. Knee that occasionally feels ready to buckle? Check. Tinnitus? check. Stiff shoulders? Check. slightly irritated left eye? check. head pain? check but I think I'm going to scale that pain down in my registry. It feels far less. I feel a bit lighter. I'm going to choose for now to focus on that, but not deny the negative feelings when they visit too. I start replaying my mom's death in all this mind circus by the way. I see her death rattles in my mind --- her long and spaced out gasps as her body let it all go—the memories of all her pains evaporating. We grow in aches. We grow in pain. We ripen up to god. I remember baptizing her in my tears as she died. I remember reading the good incantation for her spirit. I don't remember, as focused on her as I was, any of my own pains existing. I will try to focus my love on others though I know I struggle so much with it sometimes. I promise to keep growing in my love of others. My pain management plan prescribes it. Hopefully good morning and good night. I'm going to try laying down again.

Addendum 3

My Mom's Conditions and Medications

(These were copied directly from medical notes and any misspellings have been left as is.)

Diagnosis:

Type 2 diabetes mellitus with hypoglycemia without , Unspecified dementia without behavioral disturbanc , Metabolic encephalopathy , Unspecified glaucoma , Essential (primary) hypertension , Unspecified atrial fibrillation , Contracture, right wrist , Contracture, right knee , Muscle weakness (generalized) , Chronic kidney disease, stage 3 unspecified , Dysphagia, unspecified , Dysphagia, oropharyngeal phase , Difficulty in walking, not elsewhere classified , Cognitive communication deficit , Encntr for obs for susp expsr to oth biolg agents

- BACLOFEN 10 MG TABLET
- BISACODYL 10 MG SUPPOSITORY
- BRIMONIDINE 0.2% EYE DROP
- BUSPIRONE HCL 5 MG TABLET
- CITALOPRAM HBR 10 MG TABLET
- FLEET ENEMA
- HYOSCYAMINE 0.125 MG TAB SL
- LATANOPROST 0.005% EYE DROPS
- MAGNESIUM CITRATE SOLUTION
- MELATONIN 3 MG TABLET
- MILK OF MAGNESIA SUSPENSION
- POLYETHYLENE GLYCOL 3350 POWD
- TIMOLOL MALEATE 0.5% EYE DROPS
- VITAMIN B-12 1,000 MCG TABLET
- APLISOL 5T UNIT/0.1 ML VIAL
- APLISOL 5T UNIT/0.1 ML VIAL
- CARVEDILOL 12.5 MG TABLET
- DICYCLOMINE 10 MG CAPSULE
- GLIMEPIRIDE 2 MG TABLET
- LORAZEPAM 0.5 MG TABLET
- MORPHINE SULF 100 MG/5 ML CONC

- BACTROBAN 2% OINTMENT
- BACLOFEN 10 MG TABLET
- BACLOFEN 5 MG TABLET
- CITALOPRAM HBR 10 MG TABLET
- SSD 1% CREAM
- ULTRAVATE 0.05% LOTION
- TOBRAMYCIN 0.3% EYE DROP
- TRIAMCINOLONE 0.1% PASTE
- CEPHALEXIN 500 MG CAPSULE
- ACIDOPHILUS CAP(NRPK)
- TOBRAMYCIN 0.3% EYE DROP
- TOBREX 0.3% EYE OINTMENT
- BUMETANIDE 0.5 MG TABLET
- POTASSIUM CL ER 20 MEQ TABLET
- CEPHALEXIN 250 MG CAPSULE
- CEPHALEXIN 250 MG CAPSULE
- BUSPIRONE HCL 5 MG TABLET
- HALOBETASOL PROP 0.05% CREAM
- BACTROBAN 2% OINTMENT
- SSD 1% CREAM
- SSD 1% CREAM
- CEPHALEXIN 500 MG CAPSULE
- BRIMONIDINE 0.2% EYE DROP
- MUPIROCIN 2% OINTMENT
- MUPIROCIN 2% OINTMENT
- GLIMEPIRIDE 2 MG TABLET
- GLIMEPIRIDE 2 MG TABLET
- CARVEDILOL 12.5 MG TABLET
- MUPIROCIN 2% OINTMENT
- MUPIROCIN 2% OINTMENT
- CRANBERRY 450 MG TABLET
- CEFDINIR 300 MG CAPSULE
- CRANBERRY 450 MG TABLET
- CEFTRIAXONE 1 GM VIAL
- LIDOCAINE HCL 1% VIAL
- MUPIROCIN 2% OINTMENT
- CIPROFLOXACIN HCL 500 MG TAB
- CITALOPRAM HBR 10 MG TABLET
- LACTULOSE 10 GM/15 ML SOLUTION
- FLUTICASONE PROP 50 MCG SPRAY
- MUCINEX ER 600 MG TABLET

- SM GAS RELIEF 125 MG SOFTGEL
- LACTULOSE 10 GM/15 ML SOLUTION
- AMOXICILLIN 250 MG CAPSULE
- AMOXICILLIN 500 MG TABLET
- BUSPIRONE HCL 5 MG TABLET
- CITALOPRAM HBR 10 MG TABLET
- DICYCLOMINE 10 MG CAPSULE
- ENULOSE 10 GM/15 ML SOLUTION
- AMOXICILLIN 250 MG CAPSULE
- AMOXICILLIN 500 MG TABLET
- PROBIOTIC FORMULA CAP 1B-250
- AMOXICILLIN 250 MG CAPSULE
- BUSPIRONE HCL 5 MG TABLET
- CITALOPRAM HBR 10 MG TABLET
- IBUPROFEN 600 MG TABLET
- ACETAMINOPHEN 325 MG TABLET
- PROBIOTIC FORMULA CAP 1B-250
- VITAMIN C 500 MG TABLET HSTK
- BYSTOLIC 20 MG TABLET
- GLIMEPIRIDE 1 MG TABLET
- ZINC SULFATE 220 MG CAPSULE
- TIMOLOL MALEATE 0.5% EYE DROPS
- POTASSIUM CL ER 20 MEQ TABLET
- ACETAMINOPHEN 325 MG TABLET
- ACETAMINOPHEN 325 MG TABLET
- POLYETHYLENE GLYCOL 3350 POWD
- GLIMEPIRIDE 2 MG TABLET
- LATANOPROST 0.005% EYE DROPS

The Very Last Addendum

What follows is a Letter by Ram Dass. I have kept it exactly as he wrote it to parents going through a most egregious grieving process. This letter probably shaped my ability to be a death doula for my mom more than anything else. If you read back over this book carefully, you'll surely find bits and pieces of it littered along my heart's highway. I have adapted this letter many times for friends and family who are grieving. I encourage you to do the same.

Dear Steve and Anita,

Rachel finished her work on earth, and left the stage in a manner that leaves those of us left behind with a cry of agony in our hearts, as the fragile thread of our faith is dealt with so violently. Is anyone strong enough to stay conscious through such teaching as you are receiving? Probably very few. And even they would only have a whisper of equanimity and peace amidst the screaming trumpets of their rage, grief, horror and desolation.

I can't assuage your pain with any words, nor should I. For your pain is Rachel's legacy to you. Not that she or I would inflict such pain by choice, but there it is. And it must burn its purifying way to completion. For something in you dies when you bear the unbearable, and it is only in that dark night of the soul that you are prepared to see as God sees, and to love as God loves.

Now is the time to let your grief find expression. No false strength. Now is the time to sit quietly and speak to Rachel, and thank her for being with you these few years, and encourage her to go on with whatever her work is, knowing that you will grow in compassion and wisdom from this experience. In my heart, I know that you and she will meet again and again, and recognize the many ways in which you have known each other. And when you meet you will know, in a flash, what now it is not given to you to know: Why this had to be the way it was.

Our rational minds can never understand what has happened, but our hearts — if we can keep them open to God – will find their own intuitive way. Rachel came through you to do her work on earth, which includes her manner of death. Now her soul is free, and the love that you can share with her is invulnerable to the winds of changing time and space.

In that deep love, include me.

In love,

Ram Dass

About the Author

So my book is ultimately finished, but I still need to provide an "about the author" to my editor. Of course when it comes to talking about myself, I hit a writer's block. Anyone want to comment below and what you'd like to see in the author's section regarding me?

Loving son, father, mentor, teacher, and musician, traveling through life and sharing insight and inspiration with others who are open to learning and growing together. - Laura Mendez

Raw and emotionally authentic. - Loretta Shanks

Musician, teacher and writer, loving father, husband and son who accompanied his mother's last trip with love, courage, compassion and a lot of attention. Today he shares his experience with great sensitivity. - Carlos Mario Sarmiento

I once read an author interview or watched it (can't remember) where George Saunders shared his playlist that he listened to while writing his book, and ever since then, I've thought it was a really good concept. What music inspired you while writing this? What music inspires you in general? - Jess Inman

Answer to question: My mom and I listened to a lot of The Beatles in the writing of this. You'll notice mentions of them and other relevant music in the work. My mom and I also spent many hours during her last days of transition listening to Music to Die To by East Forest.

CPSIA information can be obtained
at www.ICGtesting.com
Printed in the USA
BVHW022251250922
647977BV00020B/456